THE HILLBILLY COOKBOOK
AUTHENTIC RECIPES FROM THE OLD SOUTH
HOLIDAY EDITION

Michael and Pauline Worthington

Copyright © 2011 Michael and Pauline Worthington

All rights reserved.

ISBN: 1466494840
ISBN-13: 978-1466494848

DEDICATION

First of all, this book is dedicated to my mother who got me started cooking and who made it possible for me to be here today.

Second, my wife Pauline, who not only contributed hours of typing, but has also stood by me faithfully for over 21 years through all my hare-brained schemes.

And my two beautiful daughters, Paula and Jodi, who have always been a joy to me and have always thought "Daddy" was golden.

Next is our dear friend and mentor, Willie Crawford, who never gave up on me and continually pushed me to get this thing up and going. Willie, you're the best, and we couldn't have done this without you!

Finally, all the friends and family who also contributed recipes and/or encouragement through the making of this book., this one's for you.

To all of you I offer my thanks and my undying gratitude for your love and support all these years.

What You Cookin'?

Possum tails, owl gizzards and grits fried in bear grease with goat's milk gravy, vulture eggs and mashed up catfish eyes. The catfish eyes really bring out the flavor of the possum tails.

Thanks to TV and movies written by people that don't have a clue about the south, that's the impression a lot of people get when they talk about hillbilly cooking.

Now, back in the day, people from the hills used to eat whatever was handy; mostly stuff they grew themselves, and I'm sure at some point there's been more than one unfortunate possum or 'coon made its way to the kitchen table at some point, but in truth, that's not what real southern cooking is all about.

We put this book together to give those of you that might not have the good fortune to experience the grace and beauty of authentic southern cooking the chance to see first hand just how blessed we are down here when it comes to setting a holiday table.

I actually started cooking when I was about 12 or so. My dad got disabled and couldn't work anymore so my mother went to work in a sewing factory. She wouldn't get home 'till late so it was on daddy and me to have supper ready when she got home.

Now, daddy could make cornbread and stuff, but he wasn't much for real cooking like frying chicken or pork chops, so I learned quick how to get around in the kitchen.

Since mama wasn't there to tell me no, I tried all sorts of things. I learned how to make biscuits and gravy, mashed potatoes, and one day, I decided to try baking a cake. It didn't come out too bad; maybe a little dry because I let it stay in the oven too long, but it tasted good.

That summer, I talked daddy into helping me build a makeshift barbeque pit out of rocks we wheelbarrowed up from the woods. I used an old refrigerator rack for a grill. At the time, about all I cooked on it was hotdogs and hamburgers, and maybe a chicken once in a while. It wasn't until years later I learned how to cook a steak over a flame.

In 1977 I went to work for a friend of mine in his restaurant, and that's when I discovered that I really, REALLY loved to cook. As they say, the rest is history. Pauline and I got our own restaurant about three years ago and ran it until this past summer when health and time considerations caused us to have to sell it.

So, here I am, 45 years later, and still learning every day. This book represents a small part of what I want to share and I sincerely hope you enjoy these recipes as much as I have.

Our Family
Pauline, Michael, Michael, Paula, Jiles, Jodi, Zack, and Jeff

As you can probably tell from the picture, we love to eat, and we love to cook. We sincerely hope you get as much pleasure from these recipes as we have!

CONTENTS

	Acknowledgments	i
1	Centerpieces, Appetizers, and Hors D'oeuvres	1
2	Main Courses	23
3	Sides and Veggies	39
4	Breads, Cakes, Pies, and Cookies	59
5	Drinks	131
6	About the Authors	142
7	Alphabetical Index	144
8	Family Photos	148

ACKNOWLEDGMENTS

We would like to take this opportunity to acknowledge the people who helped make this book possible and those who contributed recipes for us.

JoDanna Bell
Kelvin Brown – http://kelvinbrown.com
Willie Crawford – http://williecrawford.com
Charles Eastwood
Mary Sue Gregg
"Aunt" Pansy Hollingsworth
Kenny Russell – http://russellworkhorsefarm.com
Robbie Sanford
Paula Smith
Patricia Thomas
Harold Whiteman

To all the other friends and family who have helped or offered encouragement, this one's for you, too. Thanks from the bottom of our hearts. You guys are the best!

Michael and Pauline Worthington

CHRISTMAS IS OUR FAVORITE TIME OF YEAR

Cakes, candies, pies, baked ham and turkey...
it's enough to make a country boy's tongue
slap his brains out!

photo by Pauline Worthington

Centerpieces, Appetizers, And Hors D'oeuvres

Edible Centerpiece

Autumn Edible Centerpiece

Here's a nice centerpiece that will add that Autumn flair to any table and can double as an appetizer if you set a bowl of dip down with it.

You can substitute any of the following with your favorite produce.

6 radishes
4 green onions
1 medium pumpkin (about 8 inches in diameter)
½ medium head cabbage
1 small cucumber
6 fresh cauliflower florets
6 fresh broccoli florets
Wooden skewers
2 medium carrots, cut into 1-½ inch lengths
8 fresh green beans
6 cherry tomatoes
6 fresh asparagus spears
Toothpicks
Fresh parsley sprigs

Trim both ends of each radish. With a sharp knife, cut radishes into roses. Cut white portions of onions into 1-½ inch lengths; set aside green portions of onions for flower stems.

Cut white portions into thin strips, leaving one end intact. Place in a bowl of ice water; add radishes. Refrigerate until radishes open and onions are curled, about 30 minutes. Meanwhile, cut top off of pumpkin; scoop out and discard seeds. Place cabbage half in pumpkin, flat side down, for base.

Score cucumber by cutting lengthwise strips through peel; cut cucumber into slices. Thread the cucumber, cauliflower and broccoli onto skewers; insert into cabbage base. Drain radishes and onions, thread onto skewers and insert into base.

With a sharp knife, cut carrots into flower shapes. Thread green beans and reserved green onion portions onto skewers. Top with carrot flowers and tomatoes. Insert into base. With toothpicks, attach the asparagus to base. Fill in around inside edge of pumpkin with parsley springs (allowing them to hang over the edge of the pumpkin).

Candy Bar Race Cars

These little race cars made from candy bars make a cool centerpiece for the kids at Christmas. They're not too hard to make and will really dress up the children's table. Good for race fans for birthdays and such as well.

Chocolate-covered candy bars (Snickers or Milky Way)
Striped peppermint candies (for wheels)
Round candy-coated chocolate pieces for steering wheels like M&M's® or Skittles®

Tube or can of cake frosting (use instead of glue to stick peppermints and candy coated chocolate pieces onto miniature candy bars)

To make the driver's seat in each race car, use a butter knife to scoop out a shallow, ½-inch-wide wedge across the center of each candy bar.
Use a dab of frosting to fasten a small candy on the driver's side of the wedge for a steering wheel. Use frosting to stick peppermint candies on the sides for the wheels. Refrigerate the cars to set the frosting.

Sugared Fruit Edible Centerpiece

This isn't a main course by any means, but no holiday table is complete without an attractive centerpiece so here's one that you can eat along with all the other goodies! Easy to make and tasty as all get out. Enjoy!

Assorted whole fruit: grapes, pears, apples, plums, peaches, apricots, kumquats, bing cherries, nectarines…

2 tsp. meringue powder (found in the cake-decorating supply section of many stores

4 Tbsp. water

Superfine or granulated sugar (found in your local supermarket)

Wash all fruit. Allow it to dry on paper towels. In a 6- or 10-ounce custard cup combine the meringue powder and water. Stir with a wire whisk or fork until the powder is completely dissolved.

Place sugar in a shallow plate. Dip small fruit like cherries and kumquats into liquid and roll in sugar. Brush liquid onto larger fruits like peaches, pears, apples, and nectarines, using a pastry brush to completely moisten each piece with liquid. Set larger fruits on the plate and then spoon sugar over the fruit. Allow fruit to dry before stacking.

Candy Bar Sleds

These little candy bar sleds make an excellent centerpiece for the kids table, and can also serve for birthday parties too. It's a little bit tedious getting the candy canes and crème candies to stick, but they're worth the effort.

Small candy canes	Mellow crème toy candies
Chocolate-covered candy bars	Tube or can of cake frosting
(Snickers tm or Milky Way tm)	

Cut off ¼ inch of the curved tip on each of two candy canes. Use cake frosting to stick the canes to the bottom of the candy bar to make sled runners.

Use frosting to fasten toy candies to the top of the sled. Refrigerate the sleds to set the frosting. Don't handle the sled until the frosting is set.

Tropical Cheese Dip

1 8 oz package cream cheese, softened
1/2 cup salad dressing
1 cup shredded mild cheddar cheese

2 Tbs green onion slices
8 slices bacon, cooked crispy
½ cup crushed butter crackers

Mix cream cheese and salad dressing well, then add cheddar cheese and onions. Spoon into a 9 inch pie plate and top with crumbled bacon and cracker crumbs. Bake at 350 degrees for 15 minutes. Serve with bacon flavored crackers or Ruffles tm brand potato chips on the side. Makes 2 cups dip.

Holiday Carrot Dip

This is a dip you can make up the day before and it's really awesome since you give the herbs and spices time for the flavors to blend. Works great for any occasion.

You'll need:

1 8 oz. package Neufchatel Cheese, softened
½ cup finely shredded carrot
1 tsp. parsley flakes
1/8 tsp. salt
Dash of coarse ground black pepper

Blend everything together well and chill for 24 hours. Serve with vegetable strips or chips. Makes 1 cup dip.

Vegetable Tray with Ranch Dip

1 bag Baby Carrots, rinsed
1 head of Cauliflower (cut and rinsed Florets only)
1 bunch Broccoli (cut and rinsed Florets only)
1 package Grape Tomatoes, rinsed
2 stalks Celery, rinsed and cut into sticks
1 package Hidden Valley Ranch® Dip and ingredients listed on package

Mix Ranch Dip as directed on package, place in center of Appetizer Tray, place rinsed vegetables on the tray around the dip. Keep an extra package of Ranch Dip (and dip ingredients) in case it's needed.

From Paula Smith

Cheese and Cold Cuts Tray with Ranch Dip

3 boxes assorted crackers
1 block cheddar cheese, sliced into small squares
1 package Swiss cheese, cut into small squares
1 package pepperoni
1 package salami

2 packages Canadian bacon
½ pound smoked turkey, sliced into strips and rolled
½ pound Black Forest ham, sliced into strips and rolled
1 package dry Hidden Valley Ranch® dip and ingredients listed on package

Set crackers aside in large bowl. Mix ranch dip as directed on package, place in center of appetizer Tray, Place cheeses and cuts of meat around the dip. Keep an extra package of Ranch Dip (and dip ingredients) in case it's needed.

From Paula Smith

New Orleans Stuffed Shrimp

I've been making these since 1991 and they're always a hit. We buy shrimp down here in season right from the boat, and save the biggest ones for this. They keep well in the freezer if you put 'em in a zip lock bag and fill it with water to cover the shrimp before you freeze 'em.

1 pound raw jumbo shrimp (about 12 to 16, peeled, with tails on)
1 cup mushrooms chopped fine
1/3 cup onion chopped fine
1 clove garlic chopped fine
1 tsp chicken bouillon

1/4 cup butter or margarine
1 ½ cups soft bread crumbs (about 3 slices)
1 Tbs chopped pimiento
½ stick melted butter or margarine
2 Tbs Tony Cachere's [tm] Cajun Seasoning

Preheat oven to 400 degrees. In a large skillet, cook the mushrooms, onion, garlic, and bouillon until tender. Remove from heat and stir in Tony's tm, bread crumbs, and pimiento.

Cut a slit along the underside of each shrimp, but don't cut all the way through. Remove the vein and flatten the shrimp out. Brush the whole shrimp with melted butter or margarine, then heap the stuffing mixture into the hollow of each shrimp.

Place the shrimp in a greased, shallow baking dish and bake at 300 degrees for 10 to 12 minutes until hot. Garnish with parsley sprigs if you want. Serves 6 -8 Refrigerate the leftovers if you have any.

Holiday Ham Logs

These things are always a favorite at every holiday gathering around here. I usually make a double batch because they go so fast! The horseradish gives it a hearty zing that'll keep 'em coming back for more.

2 cups ground ham
1 egg, beaten
¼ tsp coarse ground black
   pepper
¼ cup Italian bread crumbs

½ cup horseradish sauce (below)
1 Tbs prepared mustard
1/8 tsp celery salt
Canola oil for frying
pimiento strips

Mix the ham, egg, and pepper well in a large bowl. Shape into 1 inch logs or balls and roll in bread crumbs to cover well. Refrigerate for one hour – covered.

To make the mustard sauce, mix horseradish sauce, mustard, and celery salt in a small bowl and blend well. Cover and refrigerate until time to serve it up.

In a large saucepan or dutch oven, heat about 3 inches of Canola oil until it's at least 350 degrees. You'll have to adjust the heat to maintain the temperature. Fry the ham logs for 2-3 minutes, a few at a time, until they're just golden brown and drain on paper towels. Garnish with pimiento strips and serve with the mustard sauce. Makes about 24.

Horseradish Sauce

½ cup salad dressing
2 Tbs Chili sauce
1 Tbs prepared horseradish

Mix everything together well and refrigerate. Serve with shrimp or use in Ham logs on previous page.

Bacon and Mushroom Rollups

6-8 slices bacon
1/2 lb. mushrooms, chopped
1/2 medium onion, chopped
1/2 teaspoon salt (optional)
1/8 teaspoon black pepper
1 (4 oz.) package cream cheese
12 slices bread
1/4 cup melted butter

Sauté bacon, mushrooms, onion, salt, and pepper 5 to 8 minutes. Stir in cream cheese; set aside and let cool for 15 minutes. Cut crusts from bread.

With rolling pin, flatten bread until 1/4 inch thick. Spread 2 tablespoons mushroom mixture over each slice. Roll like a jelly roll. Secure with toothpicks. Refrigerate 1 hour. Put on cookie sheet and brush with melted butter. Bake 10 to 15 minutes at 375°F until lightly brown. Cut in half and serve warm. Makes 24 appetizer-size servings.

Cajun-Baked Oysters

Down here in South Mississippi, oysters are a big thing, and these little beauties will have everybody raving about your holiday spread. You might want to make a double batch just in case!

2 dozen oysters either fresh shucked, or frozen and thawed
3 Tbs prepared horseradish
½ pound Black Forest ham (sliced ¼ inch thick and cut into strips about 3 inches long and 1 inch wide)

3 Tbs melted butter or margarine
1 Tbs lemon juice
¼ tsp garlic powder
1 Tbs Tony Cachere's tm Cajun Seasoning

Spread horseradish on one side of each strip of ham and put 1 oyster on each one. Roll it up and stick it with a toothpick. Lay them out on a broiler pan.

Mix the butter, lemon juice, garlic powder, and Tony's tm in a small bowl and brush each ham and oyster roll with some of the lemon butter. Put in the oven on broil, 5 inches away from the heat and broil for 10-15 minutes until the edges of the oysters curl. Brush every once in a while with the lemon-butter. Makes 24 appetizers.

Devilish Deviled Eggs

6 hard-boiled eggs
1/3 cup Salad Dressing or mayo
2 Tbsp. finely chopped green onion

1 tsp. prepared mustard
½ tsp. hot pepper sauce (Tabasco or Louisiana Brand)
1/8 tsp. salt

Cut eggs in half. Remove yolks; mash. Blend in remaining ingredients. Refill egg whites. Makes 12 appetizers

Stuffed Mushrooms

2 pounds medium mushrooms (about 1 ½ inch diameter)
6 Tbs margarine
1 8 oz package cream cheese

½ cup blue cheese crumbles (Get the good stuff – Kraft tm)
2 Tbs onion chopped fine

Remove the stems from the mushrooms and chop enough of them to make ½ cup. Cook the mushroom caps in 2 batches in 3 Tbs margarine on medium heat for about 5 minutes and place on cookie sheet.

Mix the cream cheese and blue cheese well, and stir in the chopped stems and onions then fill each mushroom cap with the mixture. Broil in oven 'till they're golden brown. Makes about 2 ½ dozen

Teriyaki Mini-Kabobs

1 pound boneless pork cut sliced 1 inch thick and cut into 1x4 inch strips
1 11oz can mandarin oranges
1 small green bell pepper cut into 4x1/4x1/4 inch strips

¼ cup teriyaki sauce
1 Tbs. honey
1 Tbs. apple cider vinegar
1/8 tsp. garlic powder

Soak 24 bamboo skewers in water for 10 minutes then thread the pork strips and mandarin orange sections on skewers with one pepper strip on the end of each one. Make sauce from the teriyaki sauce, honey, vinegar and garlic powder and brush over kabobs. Broil 6 inches from heat for about 15 minutes until pork is done, turning and basting every once in a while. Makes about 24.

Cheese Stuffed Tomatoes

1 cup Cottage Cheese
¼ cup (1 ounce) crumbled blue cheese (Kraft – the good stuff)
1 tsp. celery seed

1 tsp prepared mustard
¼ tsp. onion powder
30 cherry tomatoes, tops removed and seeded

In a medium bowl, combine cheeses and seasonings; mix well. Spoon cheese mixture into tomatoes; cover and chill. Refrigerate leftovers. Makes 30 appetizers.

Cheesy Potato Skins

4 large baking potatoes, baked
Canola Oil
¼ lb. Velveeta® Pasteurized Process Cheese spread, cubed
Sour Cream
2 Tbsp. chopped red or green bell pepper
2 crisply cooked bacon slices, crumbled
1 Tbsp. green onion slices

Cut potatoes in half lengthwise; scoop out center, leaving ¼-inch shell. Fry shells, a few at a time, in deep hot oil, 375°, 2 to 3 minutes or until golden brown; drain. Place on cookie sheet. Top with process cheese spread; broil until process cheese spread begins to melt. Top with remaining ingredients. Makes 8 appetizers.

Crabmeat Appetizers

1/4 lb. butter
1 5oz. jar of Cheese Whiz
1 1/2 tsp. mayonnaise
1/2 tsp. garlic salt
1 can crab meat
6 English Muffins (Hawaiian bread works well, too.)

Preheat broiler

Soften butter and cheese to room temperature. Mix together butter, Cheese Whiz, mayonnaise, garlic salt and crab meat. Spread mixture on split English muffins. Place in freezer for at least 10 minutes. Thaw just a little (about 3 minutes), cut into quarters and broil until bubbly (about 2 minutes). Serve immediately.

Alternate suggestion: Take one loaf Hawaiian bread and cut a hole in the top. Heat mixture in broiler or microwave until bubbly and pour into the hole in the bread. Tear pieces of the bread you removed from the top and spread with the crab mixture.

Cajun Chicken Nuggets

1 envelope Lipton brand Recipe Secrets onion soup mix
½ cup plain dry bread crumbs
1 ½ tsp chili powder
1 tsp. ground cumin
1 tsp. thyme
¼ tsp. red pepper
2 pounds boneless chicken breasts cut into 1 inch pieces.
Canola oil for frying
buttermilk

In a large bowl, mix onion soup mix, bread crumbs, chili powder, cumin, thyme and pepper. Dip the chicken nuggets in the buttermilk, then roll them in the bread crumb mixture. Coat well.

Heat enough Canola oil to cover the bottom of a large cast iron skillet and ease in the chicken nuggets a few at a time. Cook over medium heat, turning once until they're done. Serve warm with mustard sauce. Makes about 5 dozen nuggets.

Sausage Party Rolls

¾ pound lean ground pork or veal
¾ cup finely diced boiled potato
1 small onion, finely chopped
2 Tbsp. chopped fresh parsley
1 tsp. dried sage
1 tsp. freshly ground pepper
½ tsp. salt
¼ tsp. crushed red pepper flakes
1 (17 ¼ oz.) package frozen puff pastry sheets, thawed
Flour for dusting
1 large egg beaten
1 cup Worcestershire sauce

Preheat oven to 350° F. To make piping bag, snip one corner from a plastic food bag with scissors to make about a ¾-inch opening.

Combine pork, potato, onion, parsley, sage, ground pepper, salt, and pepper flakes in a bowl; transfer sausage mixture to plastic food bag.

Unfold one pastry sheet; following fold marks, cut the sheet into three rectangles. Cut each one in half (lengthwise to make six strips. On a lightly floured surface, roll out each strip into a 12 x 2 ½-inch rectangle. Pipe sausage mixture along one long edge of each strip. Lightly brush opposite edge with egg. Starting at edge with sausage mixture, roll up each strip, gently pressing egg-brushed edge to seal.

With a sharp knife, cut each log crosswise into eight (1 ½-inch-thick) rolls. Arrange rolls, seam side down, on a broiler pan; brush top with egg. Repeat with remaining pastry and sausage mixture.

Bake until golden brown and cooked through, 30 to 35 minutes. Serve warm with Worcestershire sauce for dipping. Makes 96 Sausage Rolls

Scandinavian Party Tray

36 slices party bread, crackers or flat bread
mayonnaise or salad dressing
36 small lettuce leaves or Belgian endive leaves
1 large can (9 ¼ ounces) Tuna, drained and flaked or broken into chunks
2 hard- boiled eggs, sliced
¼ pound frozen, cooked bay shrimp, thawed
½ medium cucumber, thinly sliced
36 pieces steamed asparagus tips or pea pods
Capers
Plain yogurt
Dill sprigs
Pimento strips
Red or black caviar
Sliced green onion for garnish

Arrange party bread on a tray; spread each with 1 teaspoon mayonnaise and/or mustard. Top with tuna, egg slices, shrimp, cucumber or steamed vegetables. Garnish as desired. Makes 36 appetizers.

Southwest Meatballs

1 ¼ pounds ground beef
1 package (1.25 ounces) Old El Paso™ taco seasoning
¼ cup unseasoned dry bread crumbs
¼ cup finely chopped onion
¼ cup finely chopped green bell pepper
1 egg, beaten
1 ½ cups chunky salsa

In a large bowl, combine all ingredients except salsa; blend well. Form into 1-inch balls. In a large skillet, brown meatballs on all sides; drain fat. Add salsa to skillet. Bring to a boil; reduce heat and simmer, uncovered, 10 minutes. Makes about 36 meatballs

Crispy Fried Mushrooms

½ cup all-purpose flour
½ tsp. salt
¼ tsp. dry mustard
¼ tsp. paprika

Dash of coarse ground black pepper
½ cup buttermilk
8 ounces whole fresh mushrooms
Canola Oil for frying

Mix flour, salt, mustard, paprika and pepper in a large plastic ziplock bag. Set aside. Place buttermilk in a small bowl. Dip a few mushrooms at a time in the buttermilk. Place in the bag with flour mixture. Shake to coat.

Heat 2 to 3 inches oil in deep-fryer or heavy saucepan to 375°. Fry a few mushrooms at a time, 2 to 3 minutes, or until deep golden brown, turning over several times. Drain on paper towels. Serve hot with catsup, if desired. Makes 4 to 6 servings.

Taco Snack Mix

This not only makes a great party tray for holiday get-togethers, but you can whip it up in a heartbeat for Superbowl parties or any other occasion. The spicy taco seasoning goes well with any drink or punch.

4 cups spoon size Shredded Wheat
4 cups pretzel sticks
4 cups tortilla chips

1 (1 ¼-ounce) package Taco Seasoning Mix
¼ cup margarine melted

In a large bowl, combine cereal, pretzels, tortilla chips and taco seasoning mix. Drizzle with margarine, tossing to coat well. Store in airtight container. Makes 12 cups

Bacon Mini-Croissants

1 8 oz package cream cheese
8 slices bacon fried crispy and crumbled
1/3 cup grated parmesan cheese
¼ cup finely chopped onion
2 Tbs. chopped fresh parsley

1 Tbs. milk
2 8oz cans refrigerated crescent rolls
1 egg, beaten
1 tsp. cold water

Pre heat oven to 375 degrees.

Beat cream cheese, bacon, onion, parsley and milk on medium speed with an electric mixer until smooth.

Separate dough into 8 rectangles and firmly press the perforations together to seal the joint. Spread each rectangle with 2 rounded measuring tablespoons of the cream cheese mix.

Cut each rectangle in half diagonally then do it again from the opposite corners. Cut in half crossways to make 6 triangles, then roll each one up starting from the short corner.

Place on greased cookie sheet and brush with mixed up egg and water. Bake 10-12 minutes or until they're golden brown. Serve while hot. Makes about 4 dozen.

Michael's Shrimp Dip

2 cans (5 oz.) tiny, broken shrimp, drained but not rinsed
1 8oz. package cream cheese, softened
2 Tbs finely chopped onion
1 Tbs garlic powder
1 tsp lemon juice
1 tsp Tony Cachere's [tm] Cajun Seasoning

Mash up shrimp with fork. Blend everything together well, and refrigerate 24 hours. Serve with bacon crackers or chips.

Spinach Dip in Hawaiian Bread

1 cup salad dressing (Miracle Whip [tm])
1 cup sour cream
1 package Hidden Valley Ranch brand dressing and dip mix
1 package frozen chopped spinach, thawed and well drained
1 can water chestnuts, drained and chopped
½ cup red bell pepper, chopped fine
1 loaf Hawaiian bread

Blend together the salad dressing, sour cream, and Hidden Valley mix then add the spinach, water chestnuts and pepper. Mix well and refrigerate.

Cut the top from the Hawaiian bread and hollow out the center. Leave the bottom crust about an inch thick. Cut the bread you take out in bite-sized pieces. Fill the hole in the bread with the spinach dip just before you're ready to serve. Arrange the bite sized pieces of bread around the loaf to eat with the dip.

BBQ Leg Quarters with homemade BBQ sauce

Here in the South, grilling isn't just a summertime event. Even in December, we're able to get together and cook out quite often.

When you love food and cooking as much as we do, there's never a bad time to grill.

Recipe on page 35

Hams, Turkeys, And Other Main Courses

Holiday Baked Ham

Baked ham has been one of the main staples of our holiday meals for at least 21 years, and I hope it will be for another 50 or so. This is one of the best methods of baking a ham we've found. We hope you like it too.

1 bone-in smoked ham (15 - 20 pounds)	1 cup apricot preserves
	1 tsp. dry mustard
1 can (20 ounces) DOLE® Sliced Pineapple in Syrup or Juice	½ tsp. ground allspice
	Whole cloves
	Maraschino cherries

Preheat oven to 300°F. Remove rind from ham. Place ham on rack in open roasting pan, fat side up. Score ham in a diamond pattern and smear it good with butter or margarine.

Insert meat thermometer with bulb in thickest part away from fat or bone. Cover ham with heavy duty aluminum foil and roast in preheated oven about 4 1/2 hours.

Drain pineapple; reserve syrup. In small saucepan, combine syrup, preserves, mustard and allspice. Bring to boil; boil, stirring occasionally, 10 minutes.

Remove ham from oven, but keep oven hot. Stud ham with cloves; brush with glaze. Using wooden picks, secure pineapple and cherries to ham. Brush again with glaze.

Return ham to oven. Roast 30 minutes longer or until thermometer registers 160°F (about 25 minutes per pound total cooking time). Brush with glaze 15 minutes before done.

Let ham stand 20 minutes before slicing.

Glazed Baked Ham

Here's another delicious method of baking a ham that our friend Harold Whiteman gave us. This one uses a half-shank portion which is good if you're only cooking for a couple of people.

1 6- to 7-lb. Fully cooked, bone-in, shank- half, smoked ham Whole cloves, for studding ham	**Glaze:** ½ cup orange marmalade 2 Tbsp. honey mustard

Pre-heat oven to 325°F. Line a 13x9-inch baking dish with aluminum foil.

Using a sharp knife, cut away tough rind on ham, making sure that you leave about ¼-inch of fat to prevent meat from drying out

With knife, lightly score top and sides of ham in a diamond pattern. Push a clove into the center of each diamond. Place ham in baking dish, with studded side up.

In small bowl stir together marmalade and honey mustard. Brush ham with half of the glaze.

Bake for one hour; brush with remaining glaze. Bake for 30 minutes loner until ham is glazed and center of ham registers 140°F.

Transfer ham to cutting board or serving platter. (If you like, the platter can be garnished with chicory or other pale greens.) Let ham stand about 20 minutes before carving. (If ham is being served to children, it's a good idea to remove cloves before serving.)

From Harold Whiteman's collection of recipes

The Best Roast Turkey Ever

Try this recipe this Thanksgiving or Christmas dinner. On the rare occasion I ever put a turkey in the oven, this is the way I do it. It takes some time, but I promise, it's worth every second.

A large turkey: 15 pounds or so
½ lb of bacon (As fatty as possible)
Salt and pepper

For the stuffing:
2 lbs pork sausage meat
2 tablespoons dried sage
1 large onion, chopped into small pieces
4 tablespoons breadcrumbs
¼ cup boiling water
Salt and pepper

Make the stuffing first thing. Combine the onion, sage and breadcrumbs together in a big bowl. Pour on the boiling water and mix this to a paste. Add the sausage meat, season with a good amount of salt and pepper and mix by hand. A lot of grocery stores make their own sausage and that's what you want to use if you can get it because they don't add all the preservatives and junk we don't want. Set the stuffing aside. Preheat the oven to 425F.

Now, wash the turkey real good, pat dry and set it on a flat surface..

Stuff the turkey at both ends. Begin with the neck end and push it up between the flesh and the skin towards the breasts. Do not pack this too tight because it will grow on you while it cooks. Tuck the neck flap under the bottom of the turkey and, if you have to, tack it with a small skewer. Put the rest in the other end.

Next, coat the turkey all over with butter. Be sure and cover it good. Next, dust it with a good amount of salt and coarse ground pepper, all over, then lay the bacon strips across the top of the turkey.

The next thing we're gonna do is wrap the turkey in foil. You'll need the wide heavy duty kind so you can cover the turkey completely and seal it up real good. You want to keep all the juices inside so it don't dry out while it bakes.

First, spread out 2 pieces of aluminum foil long enough to wrap the turkey neck to tail.

Put the edges of both pieces together longways and fold the edges several times to make one large sheet. Do this again. Now, place the turkey on one of the sheets, bend the foil up around the turkey and lay the other sheet over the top. Fold the edges over and over to seal it up.

Pick up the whole turkey, foil and all, and set it in a large roasting pan and stick it in the oven. Cook at 425F for 30 minutes and then drop the temperature down to around 325F Let it bake for another 4 to 4 ½ hours for a 20 lb turkey.

The best way to tell when it's done is with a meat thermometer. The thickest part of the breast should read 165 degrees and the juices should be clear. Be sure to stay away from the bones when you measure the temperature.

Once you get it to around 165, it's time to take off the foil and turn the oven back up to 400 degrees. Hang on to the foil, though. We're gonna need it again later. Take off the bacon and put the turkey back in the hot oven uncovered for about 30 minutes to give the skin a chance to brown and crisp. Leave it in there for about 30 – 45 minutes until the skin is a golden brown. This is where it gets a little tedious because you need to baste it every few minutes to keep it from drying out.

As soon as it's done, take the turkey out of the oven and set it on a warm cutting board. Re-cover it with the foil tent and let it set for 30 minutes or so. While it's resting, go ahead and make your gravy and the rest of the trimmings. After that, ring the dinner bell and chow down!

Deep Fried Turkey

Down here in the Deep South, most people who love to cook never put a turkey in the oven. Instead we fry them in hot oil. It takes a fraction of the time a turkey spends in a hot dry oven, and the turkey comes out tender and juicy every time. If you have the facilities, you really need to give this a try. Just be sure to do it outside, away from anything flammable. I always buy at least 2 or 3 turkeys because the first one never makes it to the dinner table.

You're gonna need:

1 or more young tom turkeys (10 – 12 pounds)

35 pounds cooking oil. Peanut oil is preferred, but it's expensive If you strain it and put it back in the container, it can be re-used several times, so it's really worth the extra money. If you can't use peanut oil for whatever reason, at least use pure vegetable.

Turkey cooker which consists of a high output gas burner w/stand and at least 30 quart pot. This time of year they're plentiful at Walmart and Sam's. You can buy a kit for about $70 that includes the pot, stand and burner, rack to hold the turkey, and lifting hook, along with a high temperature thermometer to gauge the temp of the oil.

16 oz bottle of Italian dressing

"Cajun Injector" (can be found at Walmart or Sam's and usually comes with a packet of marinate mix which I never use.)

Thaw the turkeys in the refrigerator for at least two days to make sure they're completely thawed. You don't want any ice chunks hitting the hot oil when you douse the turkey.

Set up your turkey cooker and pour in the oil, the light the fire under it on high. While the oil is heating, get the turkey(s) ready.

Remove the plastic covering and wash the turkeys thoroughly, and pat dry with paper towels inside and out. Save the giblets to use for the gravy. If it has one of those "pop-up" thermometers, take it out and dispose of it. Trim any excess skin off the neck area so it doesn't crisp around the rack and cause you to have trouble getting it loose.

Strain the Italian dressing through a tea strainer to remove all the herbs and seeds. Open the "Cajun Injector" and suck up a needle full of the oil from the dressing and inject the turkey in the thickest parts about every two inches. Start with the needle all the way in and apply pressure on the plunger as you pull it out.

Be sure to inject the breast, thighs and big parts of the legs fully. Go slow. Try to not form "pockets" of oil as you inject. Take your time and inject the whole thing gradually.

As soon as you finish the injection, place the turkey on the rack and check your oil. When it reaches 350 degrees, you're good to go.

SLOWLY lower the turkey into the hot oil using the hook provided being careful not to splash the boiling oil on you.

Cook the turkey for 3 to 3 ½ minutes per pound, making sure to keep the oil at 350 degrees. It's gonna burn on the outside, but don't worry about that. It's only the skin that's burning. Inside, where it counts, it'll be tender and juicy.

For a 10 pound turkey, pull it up after about 30 minutes and check the breast with a meat thermometer away from any bones. If it's around 165 degrees, it's done. If not, drop it back in the oil for a few more minutes. The thickest part of the breast needs to be 165 degrees to be sure you kill any nasty bacteria that might be lurking in there. The thigh needs to read around 175 – 180 degrees.

Once it's done, lift it out of the oil and dump it in a roasting pan lined with paper towels to absorb the excess oil. Let it rest for about 10 minutes before serving. Serve with giblet gravy and some herb dressing

Herb-Roasted Turkey

Here's another roast turkey recipe that Pauline's cousin, Patricia gave us. I haven't roasted this one myself, but I've tasted it at her house and it's plumb scrumptious! The herbs and vegetable stuffing helps to flavor the whole bird from the inside out.

One 14-lb. fresh or frozen turkey (thawed, if frozen)
1 medium onion, chopped
2 celery stalks, chopped
1 package poultry herb blend (fresh rosemary, thyme and sage)
½ bunch fresh parsley
1 tsp. salt, plus extra to taste
1 tsp. coarsely ground black pepper, plus extra to taste
½ tsp. dried thyme
¼ cup flour
Two 14-oz. cans chicken broth

Preheat oven to 325°F. Remove package of giblets from turkey and discard, or use to flavor gravy, if desired. Rinse turkey inside and out with cold water; drain and pat dry with paper towels.

Place onion, celery and fresh herbs inside turkey cavity. Fasten neck skin to back with skewer. With turkey breast side up, lift wings up toward neck, then fold wing tips under back of turkey so they stay in place. Tie legs together with string.

Place turkey, breast side up, on a small rack in a large roasting pan and rub all over with salt, pepper and thyme. Tent loosely with foil. Roast about 3 hours and 45 minutes; start checking for doneness during last hour of roasting.

To brown turkey, remove foil during last 1 hour and 15 minutes of roasting time and baste occasionally with pan drippings. Turkey is done when a meat thermometer inserted in the thickest part of thigh, next to the body, reads 175°F to 180°F and juices run clear when thigh is pierced with knife (breast temperature should be 165°F to 170°F). Transfer turkey to large platter; keep warm. Let stand at least 20 minutes while you make the gravy.

Pour pan drippings into a measuring cup; let it stand until the fat separates. Spoon 4 tablespoons fat into roasting pan (discard the rest of the fat). Position pan on the stovetop over medium heat and whisk in flour until golden brown, 1 minute. Gradually add reserved drippings, stirring to loosen browned bits from bottom of the pan. Whisk in chicken broth and bring to a boil. Boil, stirring frequently, 5 minutes. Season with salt and pepper to taste.

Carve turkey and serve with gravy on the side.

Deep fried turkey with stuffing on the side. Since you can't stuff the turkey before you fry it, you have to add the stuffing later.

Citrus and Herb Turkey

Pauline's step-dad was a cook on the offshore oil rigs down here for almost 20 years and here's a recipe she found while going through his cookbooks after he passed away in the late 70's. The Italian seasoning gives it a nice bouquet on the outside and the citrus, onions and herbs flavor it nicely through and through.

1 turkey (14 to 16 lbs.)	1 medium orange, quartered
¼ cup butter, softened	3 fresh rosemary sprigs
2 Tbsp. Italian seasoning	3 sprigs fresh sage
2 tsp. salt	3 cups chicken broth, divided
2 tsp. pepper	¼ cup all-purpose flour
1 large onion, quartered	Additional citrus fruits and herb
1 medium lemon, quartered	sprigs, optional

Pat turkey dry. Combine butter and Italian seasoning. With fingers, carefully loosen skin from the turkey breast; rub half of the butter under skin. Rub remaining mixture over the skin. Rub cavity with salt and pepper and fill with onion, lemon, orange, rosemary and sage. Skewer turkey openings; tie drumsticks together. Place breast side up on a rack in a roasting pan. Pour 2 cups broth into pan.

Bake at 325° for 2-¾ to 3-¼ hours or until a meat thermometer reads 180°, basting occasionally with pan drippings. Cover loosely with foil if turkey browns too quickly. Cover and let stand for 20 minutes before carving.

Pour drippings into small saucepan; skim fat. Combine flour and remaining broth until smooth; whisk into pan. Bring to a boil; cook and stir for 2 minutes or until thickened.

Discard onion, lemon, orange and herbs from the turkey; transfer turkey to a serving platter. Garnish the platter with additional citrus fruits and herb sprigs if desired.

Sausage and Grape Stuffing

One of Pauline's aunts gave us this recipe. I've tried it at Thanksgiving and Christmas get-togethers and it's really good.

1 lb. Italian sausage links (sweet and/or hot), took out of the case	2 ¾ cups water
	16-oz. pack herb stuffing mix
2 big onions, chopped up	3 cups seedless red and/or green grapes, cut in half
3 big stalks of celery chopped up	

Heat a 12-inch skillet over medium-high heat until hot. Add sausage and cook until browned, 10 minutes or so, stirring to break it up. With slotted spoon, scoop out the sausage and put it in a large bowl. Spoon the grease into a cup and set to the side.

In the same skillet, cook the onions in 1 Tbsp. sausage grease over medium heat until they start to brown, maybe about 10 minutes, stirring ever once in a while. Add onions to the bowl with the sausage.

Preheat oven to 325°F. In the same skillet, heat another 1 tablespoon drippings (throw away the rest). Add celery and ¼ cup water and cook until celery is tender, 10 minutes, stirring ever once in a while. Stir in another 2 ½ cups water and bring to a boil. Pour celery mixture over sausage mixture in bowl. Stir in stuffing mix and grapes; toss to mix well.

Spoon the stuffing into 9x13-inch glass baking dish; cover with foil and bake 20 minutes. Remove foil and bake 10 minutes longer, or until heated through and a little browned. Serves 12

Mama's Chicken and Dumplings

This chicken and dumplings recipe is at least 50 years old that I know of. I'm including it in the holiday section because ever since Pauline and I have been married, somebody always makes chicken and dumplings for holiday dinners. I used to make this for our restaurant and it sold out every time.

Large Chicken – 6-8 pounds preferably with a lot of fat
Salt and pepper
2 cups self rising flour
1 heaping tablespoon pure vegetable shortening
About a cup of buttermilk
1 16 oz can chicken stock if the chicken isn't real fat.

Put the chicken in a pot big enough to cover it with water. I use a 7 quart myself. Let it boil until it's tender, to where the meat falls off the bone when you pick it up – probably about an hour or so. Salt and pepper it to taste. About 2 tsp of each for this much water. After it boils, remove it from the water and let it cool down. Once the chicken cools, debone it and set it to the side for now.

Using the same water, check for taste and add more salt and pepper if it needs it, then bring it back to a boil.

While the chicken was boiling, you should have been making your dumplings. To do this, take about a cup of flour in a large bowl and drop in a heaping spoonful of shortening. Using a pastry blender, mix the flour and shortening until it looks like coarse ground meal. Now, pour in about ½ cup of the buttermilk and stir well, until all the flour is mixed up. It should be hard to stir with a spoon and pull away from the side of the bowl when it's right.

Now, put some more flour on a flat surface – cutting board, counter top with waxed paper, etc.. Sprinkle a little flour on top and knead it by hand a couple of times, then using a rolling pin, roll it out as thin as you can, no more than 1/8 inch thick and cut it into strips about 2" wide.

As soon as your water (stock) starts to roll, drop the dumplings one at a time into the boiling stock. Make sure it's a rolling boil so they don't stick together. When you get them all in there, take it off the heat for a few minutes to let it stop boiling, and then put it back on medium-low heat and add the deboned chicken. Let it cook down until most of the water is cooked away. Only stir occasionally so as to not break up the dumplings, but watch it so it doesn't burn.

BBQ Chicken w/Homemade Barbeque Sauce

Sauce:

1 cup ketchup
1 Med onion, chopped fine
3 Tbs fresh lemon juice
1 Tbs Olive oil
1 Tbs molasses
¼ tsp dried Thyme

1 ½ tsp Cider vinegar
1 tsp Dijon mustard
¾ tsp salt
1 clove garlic, peeled and minced
¾ tsp Tabasco ™ sauce

Mix ingredients together well and store overnight in the refrigerator in a tightly closed container.

Chicken:
Rub chicken down with olive oil and salt and pepper. Cover and refrigerate overnight. You can season with Rosemary or Thyme if you want to add a little extra flavor.

Cook on 250 degree grill about 45 minutes or until the thick part of the thigh reads 165 degrees basting with sauce occasionally.

From Paula Smith

Jambalaya

Now, you may think I'm crazy for including Jambalaya in a holiday cookbook, but here in the deep South, jambalaya is as much a staple for holiday meals as turkey or ham. This is my own recipe that I adapted from that of an old Cajun lady in Lafayette, LA back in 1981 who learned from her Grandmother. She cooked for a small eatery where I used to stop when I was working down there. I don't remember if I ever knew the lady's name but if she's still alive, she would be well over 100 years old by now.

- 2 cups long grain rice (Zatarain's if you can find it)
- 1 lb good smoked sausage (Down here we use Andouille, but it may be a little strong for you. Hillshire Farms Smoked Sausage is a great substitute for a milder flavor)
- 1 lb boneless chicken breast filets
- 1 lb peeled shrimp or crawfish – fresh or frozen (optional)
- 3 quarts water
- 1 large chopped onion
- 2 Cloves garlic minced
- 2 Tbs butter or margarine
- 2 Tbs Tony Cachere's Cajun Seasoning
- 2 Tbs thyme
- 2 Tbs paprika
- 2 Tbs chili powder (substituted for some of the peppers that are hard to find at times)
- 1 Tbs cumin
- 2 Tbs chopped parsley
- garlic powder to taste

Put the water and rice in a 12 quart pot and set on high heat to boil. While you're waiting on that, cut the sausage and chicken into 1" cubes and throw that in a large skillet with the onion and garlic. Brown the sausage and by that time, the chicken should be about half cooked and the onions turning clear. Drain off the grease from the sausage and hold back a couple of tablespoons – put that in the rice for flavor. By now the rice should be boiling nicely so go ahead and dump the sausage, chicken, onions and garlic into the water with the rice. If you're adding shrimp and/or crawfish, do it now.

Stir every once in a while to keep the rice from sticking together.

Watch it real close for a while to make sure it doesn't boil dry and burn. Add more water if you need to, but gently. You want the rice to absorb the water but you don't want it too dry. You should be able to stir it fairly easily with a long spoon, but you don't want it soupy either. If I was a real chef, I could probably explain it better, but this is the best I can do.

Making Jambalaya is more an art form than a science because everybody makes it different, and most everybody's got a different taste they like. You'll just have to experiment with it to find yours.

You'll notice I didn't tell you to add salt. That's because the Tony Cachere's has a bunch of salt in it already, and a little Tony's goes a long way especially for the uninitiated.

Now, when the rice has cooked and most of the water has been absorbed, taste it see if it needs anything. If you want a little more zing to it, and maybe it needs a little salt, add some more Tony's. If all it needs is salt, then add a pinch. If it's salty enough, but you'd like a little more spice, add a dash of Cayenne pepper, but BE CAREFUL! A little cayenne goes a long way. A lot of times, I find it needs a little more garlic, so I add a touch of garlic powder. It all depends on your particular taste and what you think is good.

I've eaten a lot of Jambalaya since I moved to Mississippi in the 80's and this recipe is one of the best I've found. I don't like it so hot it burns the hair off your tongue while you're trying to eat it, but I do like it spicy and I think I've found a happy medium that most people can live with. If your hair sweats while you're eating, but your tongue is Ok, then it's just about right. I know when I made it at the restaurant, I very rarely had to worry about what to do with the leftovers.

Pork Chops with Rice and Gravy

This isn't exactly a holiday recipe, but it's great anytime, and I felt led to include it in this book. We made this at the restaurant and always had good success with it. We rarely had leftovers to deal with. I cut the chops thicker to keep them from cooking to pieces, but you may want to adjust the cooking time and cut your chops a little thinner.

½ boneless pork loin cut in ¾ inch chops (about 5 pounds)
1 cup sour cream
2 large cans Cream of Mushroom soup
1 small can Cream of Celery soup
1 package Liptons^{tm} Golden Onion dry soup mix
½ cup milk
4 cups cooked rice
Butter or margarine to coat bottom of pan

Spread butter or margarine over bottom of a large roasting pan and layer the bottom with the chops (the less layers the better). Mix all the soup, sour cream and soup mix together with the milk and pour over the chops making sure they're well covered with the gravy.

Only if you must; add another small can of cream of mushroom soup to make more gravy before you put it in the oven.

Put the cover on the roasting pan and bake in 350 degree oven for about 2 to 3 hours, then check for doneness. The chops are done when you can pull them apart with a fork. Once they're done, serve them directly from the pan over cooked rice. They go well with garlic bread made from Texas Toast brushed with melted margarine, dusted with garlic powder and browned on the griddle or in a large cast iron skillet. Add some green peas and corn on the side and Mmmmm, Mmmm!

SIDES AND VEGGIES

Santa with Miss Kitty and White Socks

Baby Lima Beans with Onions

One day Mr. Harold Whiteman was visiting us at the restaurant and we were serving baby lima beans as one of the sides. We got to talking and he said "you know, these beans are good, but I've got a recipe that'll knock your socks off." I told him I'd sure like a copy of it because baby limas are one of my favorite beans. The next time he came in, here's what he brought, and you know what? He was right! As a bonus, it's quick and easy to make too.

1 package (10-oz.) frozen baby lima beans
2 Tbsp. olive oil
2 medium celery stalks with leaves, finely chopped
1 small red onion, finely chopped
1 large garlic clove, minced
1 Tbsp. white wine vinegar
2 tsp. minced fresh parsley
¼ tsp. salt
1/8 tsp. coarsely ground black pepper

In 10-inch skillet, prepare frozen baby lima beans as label directs. Drain lima beans well and set aside. Wipe skillet dry.

In same skillet, heat olive oil over medium heat. Add celery with leaves, onion, and garlic and cook 10 minutes or until vegetables are tender, stirring occasionally. Add cooked lima beans, vinegar, parsley, salt, and pepper; heat through. Makes 4 accompaniment servings

From Harold Whiteman's collection of recipes

Bacon and Egg Potato Salad

I'm not sure where we got this recipe, but it was a good seller in our restaurant. The green onions and paprika give it a Christmasy look.

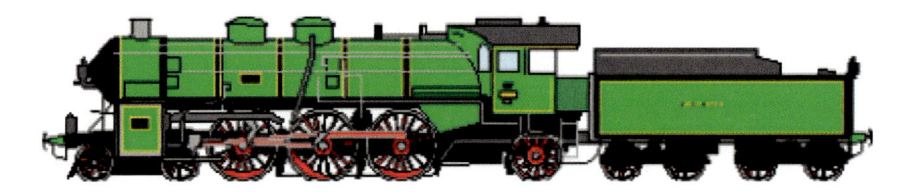

5 cups cooked, peeled and cubed potatoes (about 2 pounds)
¼ cup chopped green onions
1/3 cup lemon juice
1/3 cup water
¼ cup vegetable oil
1 ½ tsp. celery salt
1 tsp. Worcestershire sauce
½ tsp. dry mustard
¼ tsp. pepper
4 slices bacon, cooked and crumbled
3 hard-boiled eggs, chopped
¼ cup grated Parmesan cheese
3 Tbsp. chopped parsley
Paprika

In large bowl, combine potatoes and onions. In small saucepan, combine lemon juice, water, oil, celery salt, Worcestershire, mustard and pepper; bring to a boil. Pour over potato mixture; mix well. Cover; chill overnight to blend flavors. Remove from refrigerator 30 minutes before serving; stir in bacon, eggs, Parmesan cheese and parsley. Top it off with paprika. Refrigerate leftovers if you have any. Makes 10 to 12 servings

Candied Sweet Potatoes

I think maybe one of Pauline's aunts gave us this recipe a few years ago. I can't remember which one, but it sure is good. No holiday meal is complete without candied sweet 'taters and this one is a winner for sure.

4 lbs. sweet potatoes (about 8 medium), peeled and cut into 1 ½-inch chunks
½ cup packed brown sugar
4 Tbsp. butter
¾ tsp. salt
1 ½ tsp. vanilla extract
¼ cup slivered almonds (optional)

Preheat oven to 425°F. Grease a 9x13-inch glass or ceramic baking dish. Place potatoes in prepared baking dish; cover with foil and bake 20 minutes. Meanwhile, in a 1-quart saucepan, combine brown sugar, butter and salt. Cook over medium heat, stirring frequently, until mixture comes to a simmer. Simmer 1 minute. Remove saucepan from heat and stir in vanilla. Keep warm.

Remove baking dish from oven. Spoon brown-sugar mixture evenly over potatoes and stir to coat. Bake, uncovered, 40 to 45 minutes longer, or until potatoes are tender and glazed, basting with juices in pan halfway through baking. Remove baking dish from oven and let potatoes stand 10 minutes before serving. If you want, top with slivered almonds. Serves 12

Creamy Corn Pudding

Back in the old days, meaning in the 50's and 60's, you made meals based on what you grew mostly. Since most people back then had cows and chickens, and we grew corn every year, the ingredients for this recipe were usually handy. It's been updated a bit with some modern day ingredients. Now, if you have the same reaction I had, it's not going to sound good at all, but give it a try. I think you'll be pleasantly surprised!

2 eggs, lightly beaten
2 Tbsp. butter or margarine, melted
2 cups low-fat milk
1 ear fresh corn or 1 4-oz. can whole kernel corn, rinsed and drained

1 (17-oz.) can cream-style corn
1 tsp. salt
1/8 tsp. black pepper (coarse ground)
½ tsp. butter or margarine

Preheat oven to 350°F. In a large bowl, combine the eggs, butter, and milk. Add the corn, salt, and pepper; mix well.

Spread a 1 ½-quart baking dish with the ½ teaspoon butter. Pour the corn mixture into the pan. Place the dish in a larger pan. Add enough water to the pan to come halfway up the sides of the baking dish.

Bake about 50 to 60 minutes or until lightly browned and a knife inserted in the center come out clean. Serves 4 to 6

From Harold Whiteman's collection of recipes

Stuffed Acorn Squash

If you like squash, you're gonna love this! I tried this last year at the family Thanksgiving soirée and had to have the recipe.

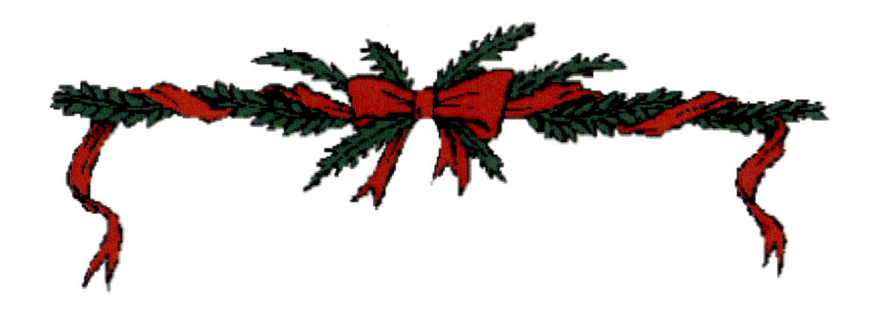

1 (13 ¾-fluid ounce) can Beef or Chicken Broth
2 small acorn squash, halved and seeded
1/3 cup margarine
2 cups dry herb-seasoned stuffing mix
1 (2-ounce) package Pecan Pieces
1/3 cup seedless raisins

Reserve 2/3 cup broth; pour remaining broth into shallow baking dish. Place squash cut-side down in broth. Bake at 400°F for 25 – 35 minutes. In medium saucepan, over medium-high heat, heat reserved broth and margarine until margarine melts; stir in stuffing mix, pecans and raisins. Turn squash over, cut-side up; spoon stuffing into squash cavities. Bake 20 minutes more or until squash is done, basting with broth after 10 minutes.

Makes 4 servings

Carrot Raisin Salad

2 to 3 medium carrots, shredded*
(1 ½ cups)
1 4 cup canned crushed
   pineapple, drained

1 Tbsp. mayonnaise
4 lettuce leaves
¼ cup raisins

*Packaged shredded carrots are available in the produce section, but this recipe is better with freshly shredded carrots. They need to be shredded finer than the commercial kind.

Combine carrots, raisins, pineapple and mayonnaise in large bowl. Refrigerate 2 hours, stirring occasionally.

Serve on lettuce leaves. Makes 4 servings

Glazed Baby Carrots

5 bunches baby carrots (1 pound without tops), peeled, or 1 16oz bag peeled baby carrots
2 Tbsp. margarine or butter (¼ stick)
1 garlic clove, cut in half
3 Tbsp. pure maple syrup or maple-flavor syrup
1/8 tsp. coarsely ground black pepper
1 Tbsp. snipped fresh chives for garnish

In 3-quart saucepan, heat 8 cups water to boiling over high heat. Add carrots and 2 teaspoons salt; heat to boiling. Reduce heat to low; cover and simmer 7 minutes or until carrots are tender. Drain well.

In nonstick 12-inch skillet, melt margarine or butter over medium heat. Add garlic and cook 2 minutes, stirring occasionally. With slotted spoon, remove and discard garlic. Add maple syrup, stirring to blend with melted margarine or butter.

Add carrots, pepper, and ¼ teaspoon salt and cook, stirring occasionally, until carrots are lightly browned, about 10 minutes. Garnish with snipped chives to serve. Makes 4 servings

From the Harold Whiteman collection of recipes

Green Bean, New Potato and Ham Salad

This isn't exactly a holiday dish in the traditional sense, but it always goes over well at our get-togethers. There never seems to be any leftovers to worry about!

3 pounds new potatoes, quartered (out of season? Use regular red potatoes cut in 1/2" cubes)
2/3 cup cold water
1 pound green beans, cut in half

¾ cup salad dressing (or mayo)
1/3 cup stone ground mustard
2 Tbsp. red wine vinegar
2 cups cubed Ham
½ cup chopped green onions

Place potatoes and 1/3 cup water in 3-quart microwave-safe casserole; cover.

Microwave on HIGH 13 minutes or until tender. Stir in beans. Microwave 7 to 13 minutes or until tender; drain.

Mix salad dressing, mustard and vinegar in large bowl until well blended. Add potatoes, beans and remaining ingredients; mix lightly. Refrigerate. Makes 12 cups

Autumn Casserole

This recipe from Harold Whiteman is an awesome addition to any holiday table. I prefer the plain old yellow crookneck squash myself, but it's good with just about any kind. The cornflakes and pecans give it a hearty crunch that makes up for the mushy cooked squash.

Topping:

4 tsp. sugar
3 cups cornflakes, coarsely crumbled
¾ cup pecans, chopped
4 Tbsp. butter, melted

Apple Mixture:

6 to 7 large cooking apples, peeled, cored and sliced (not too thin)
4 tsp. granulated sugar
2 ½ Tbsp. butter

Squash Mixture:

6 cups fresh or frozen cubed butternut or other dry squash, boiled until tender (about 12 minutes)
4 Tbsp. butter
2 Tbsp. brown sugar
¼ tsp. salt

Preheat oven to 350°F. Mix topping ingredients in a bowl; set aside.
Prepare apples: Heat 2 ½ tablespoons butter in a skillet over medium heat. Add apples and sauté for about 3 minutes, or until tender. Stir in granulated sugar. Transfer to a glass or ceramic 9x13-inch baking pan, spreading apples evenly.
Prepare squash: In a bowl, mash cooked squash with 4 tablespoons butter, the brown sugar and salt. Spread the squash evenly over the apples. Sprinkle the cornflake topping over the squash.
Bake for 20 minutes, or until topping is golden brown and crunchy.
Serves 8
From the Harold Whiteman collection

Canopy Club Squash Casserole

This squash recipe is one we used at the restaurant and always got a good response from it. I had to scale it down from the original that we used so I hope I got all the measurements right.

- 8 cups sliced young yellow crookneck squash, cooked and drained
- 6 slices bacon, cooked crispy and crumbled
- 1 lb good smoked sausage (we like Hillshire Farms™)
- 2 eggs
- 1 cup cottage cheese (or softened cream cheese if you prefer)
- 2 Tbsp. flour
- 2 tsp. Chicken-Flavor Instant Bouillon
- 1 cup (4 ounces) shredded sharp Cheddar cheese

Slice the smoked sausage diagonally in about 3/8 in. slices and brown in a skillet. Drain on paper towels to soak up grease.

Preheat oven to 350°F. In large bowl, combine eggs, cottage cheese, sausage, flour and bouillon. Add squash; mix well. Turn into greased 12x7-inch baking dish. Top with Cheddar cheese and bacon. Bake 20 to 25 minutes. Let stand 5 minutes before serving. Refrigerate leftovers if you have any.

Makes 6 to 8 servings

Red Beans and Rice

There's never a family round up down here without red beans and rice. This is the recipe we used at the restaurant and I always have to make it anytime we all get together. I put it in the "sides" section, but it's actually a meal in itself.

2 lbs Light red kidney beans soaked overnight
4 cups long grain rice - cooked (Zatarains if you can find it)
1 lb ground chuck
1 lb smoked sausage sliced diagonally in 3/8 in. slices
4 Tbs butter or margarine
1 large onion chopped fine
½ cup green bell pepper chopped fine
2 Tbs minced garlic
½ cup chopped celery
1 large or 2 small bay leaves
2 Tbs sweet basil leaves
Garlic powder to taste
2 Tbs Paprika
2 Tbs chili powder
1 Tbs cumin powder
2 Tbs parsley flakes
2 Tbs Tony Cachere's™ Cajun Seasoning

Put the beans on to boil in a 12 quart pot. Then in a large skillet, brown the ground chuck and dip it out with a slotted spoon and drain on paper towels to soak up the grease. Brown the sausage and go ahead and dump it in the beans along with the ground chuck. Don't worry about soaking up all this grease because we want a little of it to help flavor the beans.

Next, melt the butter or margarine in the skillet and put in the onion, garlic, bell pepper, and celery. Saute' until they're tender – about 10 minutes or so.

Once this is done, dump it in the boiling beans with the rest of the spices. Boil for about 45 minutes and check to see if the beans are getting tender. Add a little water if you have to, just don't let them boil dry. When they get done, serve over rice. I usually end up adding a little garlic powder, and maybe a touch of salt before they get done. If you want a little more spice, add a dash of cayenne pepper, but be careful! A little goes a long way to heat things up.

Aunt Pansy's Chicken and Dumplings

This is without a doubt the absolute best chicken and dumplings in the world, and I've traveled a good bit of it. Pauline's Aunt Pansy makes this every time we get together for any reason. I think most of the family shows up just for her chicken and dumplings. The secret is in the dumplings.

Chicken:
1 large baking hen – 6-8 lbs
2 Chicken flavored bouillon cubes
4 quarts water
salt and pepper to taste

Dumplings:
Self-rising flour (quantity depends on how many dumplings you want to make)
cold water

Put the chicken on to boil with enough water to keep it covered. Add bouillon cubes and salt and pepper. Cover with a lid and bring to a boil.

Boil chicken for about an hour to an hour and a half (take the lid off if it begins to boil over). With a fork, check to see if the meat will pull off the bones easily. You want the bones to be clean when you debone it.

Keep watch on the water as it boils and add more if you need to. When your chicken gets done, take it out of the stock and debone it, return the chicken to the stock. Bring the stock back to a rolling boil.

To make the dumplings, pour flour into a large bowl, make a hole in the center with the back of your fingers, leaving flour in bottom of bowl. Add **water** (as needed) and knead with clean hands until mixed. You want the batter to be **thick**. Make a ball and dust with flour until dough is no longer sticky, pinch off a little dough, dust with flour and roll it like you would a biscuit, place on a floured board; with a rolling pin, roll the dough out until it is almost paper thin. Dust with flour as needed. Cut into 2 inch strips.

Add the dumplings one at a time until you get them all in there. On occasion, you may need to gently dunk the dumplings (with a wooden spoon) into the broth as you drop them into the boiling stock. Reduce the heat to low, cover and simmer until the dumplings are done and most of the broth cooks away. Keep watch on it so it doesn't burn, and only GENTLY stir occasionally so the dumplings don't break up.

Pauline's Holiday Dressing

Cornbread for Dressing

4 cups Martha White self-rising corn meal mix
2 large eggs

2 2/3 cups buttermilk
2 large onions, peeled and chopped

Dressing

1 Baking hen, 6-8 lbs, boiled and deboned (save broth)
2 pones cornbread (1 - 10" iron skillet and 1 - 8")
1 dozen large boiled eggs, peeled and chopped

2 Quarts chicken broth
1-2 loaves stale white bread
1 Tbs garlic powder
salt and pepper to taste

Remove giblets from the chicken. Cover with water and boil chicken and giblets until done and the meat comes off the bone easily. Debone as soon as it's cool enough to handle. Set aside.

Preheat oven to 450 degrees. Cover bottom of a 8" and a 10" cast iron skillet with cooking oil and heat on top of stove. Remove from heat.

Mix above (Cornbread) ingredients together. Add cooking oil from each skillet to mixture and mix well.

Bake about 20 minutes until golden brown and toothpick inserted into center of each pone of cornbread comes out clean. The larger skillet may need to bake a few minutes longer.

Crumble cornbread bread into a large 11 x 15 inch roasting pan. Crumble white bread (end pieces and all), mix with cornbread, add the eggs, chicken, and chicken broth (from chicken), garlic powder, salt and pepper. Mixture should be very juicy. If it is not juicy enough, add can chicken broth. Mix well. Let the bread soak up the chicken broth.

Bake at 350 degrees until dressing is no longer juicy (but moist) and has turned golden brown; at least an hour or more, checking every once in a while to make sure it's not drying out too much.

Giblet Gravy

Dice giblets fine and set aside.

In a cast iron skillet, cover bottom with cooking oil, when it gets hot, add about one to two tablespoons flour, fry (stirring constantly) until flour gets dark brown. Add two to three cups chicken broth (be careful of the steam, don't get burnt). Stir until flour is dissolved, then add giblets, salt, garlic powder, and pepper to taste. Bring to a boil stirring constantly, reduce heat and let simmer about 3 to 5 minutes so the gravy thickens, stirring as needed, then remove from heat.

For those who don't like giblet gravy... (to make 2 cups gravy); combine ¼ cup Chicken gravy mix and ¼ cup Turkey gravy mix, with 2 cups water in a 2 quart sauce pan or cast iron skillet. Add salt and pepper taste. Bring to a boil, stir as needed, reduce heat and simmer 3 to 5 minutes.

Serve dressing with homemade giblet gravy, turkey and sliced cranberry sauce.

Pauline Worthington

Mama's Cornbread Dressing

I found this recipe in my Mom's Cookbook. I don't know where she got it, but it's at least 57 years old! I've been eating this dressing since I was a little kid.

1 baking hen – about 5 pounds
2 pones cornbread, crumbled
  (baked in 10" cast iron skillet)
Large onion, chopped
1 cup celery, chopped
butter for sautéing onions and
  celery
chicken broth

turkey broth
4 boiled eggs – chopped
poultry seasoning to taste
fresh sage, chopped
salt and pepper to taste

Boil chicken until tender and debone. Set aside for now.

Crumble cornbread. Cook onion and celery in butter until tender. Add the vegetables to the cornbread. Mix together some chicken broth and turkey broth, 4 eggs, and season with poultry seasoning and sage to taste then mix it all together with the deboned chicken.

Dump it all in a large roasting pan and bake at 350 ° for 55 to 60 minutes. After about 45 minutes or so, check the moisture in the dressing. It will dry out as it bakes and you don't want it to get too dry.

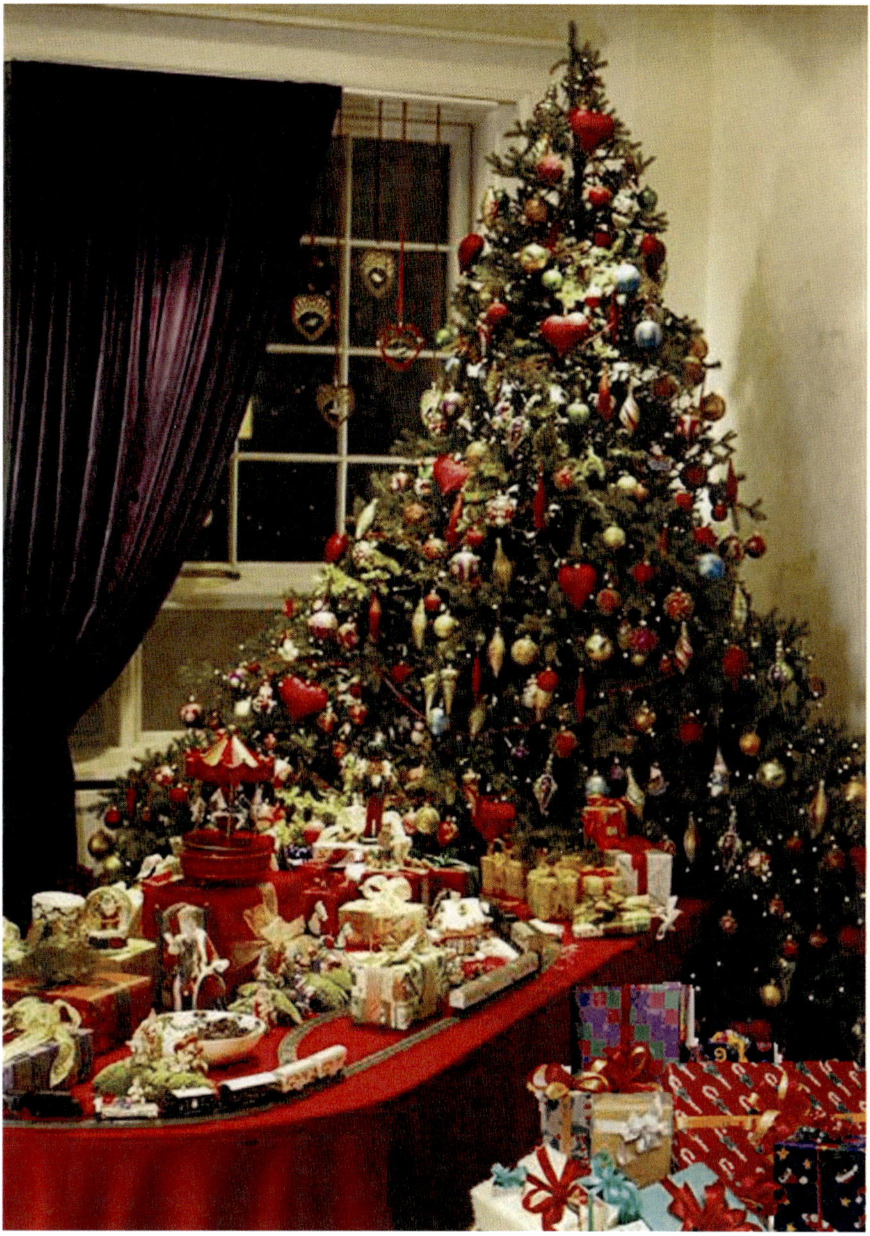

Ho…Ho…Horsey!

BREADS, CAKES PIES AND COOKIES

Aunt Pansy's Carrot Cake

Christmas dinner just ain't Christmas dinner without Aunt Pansy's Carrot Cake. So moist you can almost wring the juice out of it, and a taste to die for. Pauline's Aunt Pansy has been making this cake for over 50 years and it's another reason for the family to show up at Thanksgiving or Christmas..

Preheat Oven to 250 or 300 degrees (depending on how your oven bakes)

3 cups Wesson (vegetable oil)
6 eggs
3 cups self-rising flour
3 cups sugar
1 tsp. cinnamon
1 cup shredded carrots
1 cup pecans (or other nuts)
2 tbsp. vanilla

Place all ingredients in a large mixing bowl and blend with a wire whisk just until blended together. DO NOT OVERBEAT. Pour batter equally into 3 round 9" cake pans and bake at 250 – 300 degrees until done. When the cake starts to brown, and a toothpick inserted in the center comes out clean, it's done. DO NOT OVERBAKE. Cool completely before frosting.

FROSTING:

1 8 oz package cream cheese – softened
½ stick butter – softened
1 – 1 ½ pounds powdered sugar
1 tsp vanilla

Mix cheese, butter and vanilla together in a large mixing bowl and add sugar while mixing until it's thick enough to stay on the cake.

Mama's Pumpkin Pie

This is the way my mother made her pumpkin pie when I was a kid – updated with a few of my own notes.

- Basic pie dough or crust (you can use the store-bought ones if you want)
- 2 cups cooked pumpkin or canned pumpkin (unsweetened and mashed up well so no lumps)
- 2/3 cup brown sugar
- 1/3 cup sugar
- 1 Tbsp. all-purpose flour
- ½ tsp. salt
- 1½ tsp. ground cinnamon
- ¼ tsp. allspice or pumpkin pie spice
- ½ tsp. nutmeg
- ½ tsp. ginger
- Pinch of ground black pepper or (my favorite) white pepper
- 1 cup heavy cream (this was plentiful back in the day – now you have to buy it)
- 1 8 oz package cream cheese (Mama used cottage cheese – I prefer cream cheese)
- 2 large eggs
- 3 tbsp. rum
- 1½ tsp. vanilla

Preheat oven to 400°F. Prebake the crust for 8 minutes with edges covered in foil so they don't over-brown during the baking.

Whisk together all the ingredients and pour into the prebaked shell. Bake for 45 minutes. The center should be a little wobbly, but set. Serve with REAL whipped cream. (page 62)

Sweet Potato Pie

I much prefer pumpkin pie to sweet potato, but this one almost makes a convert out of me. It's delicious and well worth the trouble!

1 pound sweet potatoes,* boiled and peeled
¼ cup (½ stick) butter or margarine
1 (14-ounce) can EAGLE BRAND® Sweetened Condensed Milk (NOT evaporated milk)
2 eggs
1 tsp. grated orange rind
1 tsp. vanilla extract
1 tsp. ground cinnamon
1 tsp. ground nutmeg
¼ tsp. salt
1 (9-inch) unbaked pie crust

* For best results, use fresh sweet potatoes.

Preheat oven to 350°F. In large bowl, beat sweet potatoes and butter until smooth. Add EAGLE BRAND®, eggs, orange rind, vanilla, cinnamon, nutmeg and salt; mix well. Pour into crust.
Bake 40 minutes or until golden brown. Cool. Garnish as desired. Serve with the whipped cream below. Makes 1 (9-inch) pie

Real Whipped Cream

1 cup heavy cream or whipping cream
sugar to taste (about 3-4 Tbs)
1 tsp vanilla extract

Mix together sugar, vanilla, and cream in large bowl and mix on medium-high speed until it forms stiff peaks. Serve with pumpkin pie or sweet potato pie.

Quick and Easy Pecan Pie

1 – 9" deep dish pie crust
1 cup light Karo syrup
4 eggs

1 cup pecan halves
1 cup brown sugar

Mix all ingredients and pour into pie shell. Bake at 425°F for 5 minutes, reduce heat to 325°F for 1 hour.

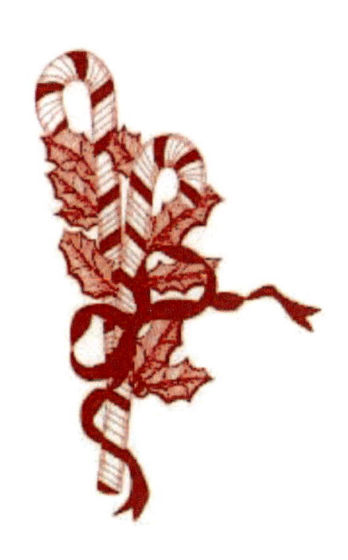

Classic Apple Pie

1 package (15 ounces) refrigerated pie crusts
6 cups sliced Granny smith, Crispin or other firm-fleshed apples (about 6 medium)
½ cup sugar
1 Tbsp. cornstarch
2 tsp. lemon juice

½ tsp. ground cinnamon
½ tsp. vanilla
1/8 tsp. salt
1/8 tsp. ground nutmeg
1/8 tsp. ground cloves
1 Tbsp. whipping cream

Preheat oven to 350°F. Line 9-inch pie pan with 1 pie crust. (Keep remaining pie crust in refrigerator until ready to use.)

Combine apples, sugar, cornstarch, lemon juice, cinnamon, vanilla, salt, nutmeg and cloves in large bowl; mix well. Pour into prepared crust. Place second crust over apples; crimp edge to seal.

Cut 4 slits in top crust; brush with cream. Bake 40 minutes or until crust is golden brown. Cool slightly before serving.

Cranberry Cobbler

This isn't typically an old South recipe, but it's good and I wanted to include it in the book. It's from the Harold Whiteman collection

- 1 package DUNCAN HINES® Moist Deluxe Yellow Cake Mix
- ½ tsp. ground cinnamon
- ¼ tsp. ground nutmeg
- 1 cup (2 sticks) butter or margarine, softened
- ½ cup chopped nuts
- 1 can (21 ounces) peach pie filling
- 1 can (16 ounces) whole cranberry sauce
- Vanilla ice cream or real whipped cream

Preheat oven to 350°F.

Combine dry cake mix, cinnamon and nutmeg in bowl. Cut in butter with pastry blender or two knives until crumbly. Stir in nuts; set aside.

Combine peach pie filling and cranberry sauce in ungreased 13x9x2 inch pan; mix well. Sprinkle crumb mixture over fruit.

Bake at 350°F for 45 to 50 minutes or until golden brown. Serve warm with ice cream or whipped cream on page 74. Makes 16 servings.

Honey-Date Pumpkin Cookies

¾ cup butter, softened
1 1/3 cups sugar
¼ cup honey
1 egg
1 cup canned pumpkin
1 tsp. milk

2 ½ cups all-purpose flour
1 tsp. baking powder
¾ tsp. salt
¾ cup chopped dates
¾ cup chopped pecans
2 Tbsp. poppy seeds

Frosting:
1 pkg. (3 oz.) cream cheese, softened
¼ cup butter, softened

2 cups confectioners' sugar
2 Tbsp. heavy whipping cream
1 tsp. vanilla extract

In a large bowl, cream butter and sugar until light and fluffy. Gradually beat in honey and egg. Add pumpkin and milk; mix well. Combine the flour, baking powder and salt; gradually add to creamed mixture and mix well. Stir in the dates, pecans and poppy seeds.

Drop by rounded tablespoonfuls 2 inches apart onto greased baking sheets. Bake at 350° for 12 to 15 minutes or until edges are lightly browned. Remove to wire racks to cool completely.

For frosting, In a large bowl, beat the cream cheese, butter and confectioners' sugar until light and fluffy. Beat in cream and vanilla until smooth. Frost cookies. Store in an airtight container in the refrigerator. Yield: 5 dozen

Easy Rocky Road Bars

2 cups (12-oz. pkg.) HERSHEY'S® Semi-Sweet Chocolate Chips
¼ cup (½ stick) butter or margarine

2 Tbsp. shortening
3 cups miniature marshmallows
½ cup chopped nuts

Butter 8-inch square pan. In large microwave-safe bowl, place chocolate chips, butter and shortening. Microwave at HIGH (100%) 1 to 1 ½ minutes or just until chocolate chips are melted and mixture is smooth when stirred. Add marshmallows and nuts; blend well. Spread evenly in prepared pan. Cover; refrigerate until firm. Cut into 2-inch squares. Makes 16 squares.

Easy Rocky Road Bars

Herb - Parmesan Bread

5 ¼ to 5 ¾ cups all-purpose flour
2 packages active dry yeast
1 tsp. salt
¼ tsp. garlic powder
2 cups warm water (120° to 130°)
Cornmeal

1 cup grated Parmesan cheese
2 tsp. fines herbes, crushed
1 slightly beaten egg white
1 Tbsp. water

In a large mixing bowl stir together 2 cups of the flour, the yeast, salt, and garlic powder. Add the warm water. Beat with an electric mixer on low to medium speed for 30 seconds, scraping the sides of the bowl constantly. Then beat on high speed for 3 minutes. Using a wooden spoon, stir in as much of the remaining flour as you can.

Turn the dough out onto a lightly floured surface. Knead in enough of the remaining flour to make a stiff dough that is smooth and elastic (8 to 10 minutes total). Shape dough into a ball. Place the dough in a lightly greased bowl, turning once to grease the surface. Cover and let rise in a warm place till double in size (1 to 1 ½ hours).

Punch dough down. Turn out onto a lightly floured surface. Divide dough in half. Cover and let dough rest for 10 minutes. Lightly grease a large baking sheet. Sprinkle with cornmeal.

On a lightly floured surface, roll each portion of dough into a 15x12-inch rectangle. In a small mixing bowl stir together the Parmesan cheese and fines herbes. Sprinkle ½ cup of the cheese mixture over each dough rectangle to within 1 inch of the edges. Roll up each rectangle, jelly-roll style, starting from one of the long sides. Moisten edges and pinch seams to seal well. Taper ends.

Place the loaves seam sides down on the prepared baking sheet. Cover the loaves with a damp cloth and let them rise till *nearly* double (about 45 minutes).

Stir together the egg white and the 1 tablespoon water. Brush some of the egg white mixture over each loaf. Using a very sharp knife, make 5 or 6 diagonal cuts, about ¼ inch deep, across the tops of the loaves. Bake in a 375° oven for 40 to 45 minutes* or till loaves sound hollow when tapped with the tip of your finger (if necessary; cover loaves loosely with foil the last 15 minutes of baking to prevent overbrowning). Remove loaves from baking sheet and cool on a wire rack.

Makes 2 loaves.

*For a crispier crust, after 20 minutes of baking, brush loaves again with the egg white mixture.

To freeze: Cool loaves completely, then wrap tightly in *heavy* foil or place in freezer bags or containers. Seal, label, and freeze for up to 3 months. Thaw the wrapped loaves at room temperature for 1 hour.

Herb-Parmesan Bread

Buttery Pecan Caramels

2 cups sugar
2 cups half-and-half (1 pint)
¾ cup light corn syrup
½ cup real butter

½ cup semi-sweet real chocolate chips, melted
64 pecan halves

In 4-quart saucepan combine sugar, 1 cup half-and-half, corn syrup and butter. Cook over medium heat, stirring occasionally, until mixture comes to a full boil, 7 to 8 minutes. Add remaining 1 cup half-and-half; continue cooking, stirring often, until candy thermometer reaches 245°F or small amount of mixture dropped into ice water forms a firm ball, 35 to 40 minutes. Pour into buttered 8-inch square pan. Cover; refrigerate 1 to 1 ½ hour to cool. Cut into 64 pieces. Drop ¼ tsp. melted chocolate on top of each caramel; press pecan half into chocolate. Cover; store refrigerated.

Makes 64 caramels

Cranberry Candy

Melt 1 ½ cups semisweet, dark, or white chocolate chips in the microwave. Stir in ½ cup almonds and ½ cup dried cranberries. Drop by teaspoonfuls onto a cookie sheet lined with parchment paper and let harden at room temperature.

From the Harold Whiteman Collection of recipes

Patricia's Divine Divinity

3 cups granulated sugar	2 egg whites
1/2 cup light corn syrup	1 tsp vanilla extract
2/3 cup warm water	1 cup chopped pecans or walnuts

Line a cookie sheet with foil and spray it down with cooking spray.
Combine the sugar, corn syrup and water in a large heavy-bottomed saucepan over medium heat. Cook, stirring constantly, until the sugar dissolves. Continue cooking without stirring until the mixture reaches 250 degrees, firm-ball stage.
Beat the egg whites in the bowl of a large standing mixture until stiff peaks form. Slowly pour about half of the sugar syrup into the egg whites, beating constantly.
Continue to cook the remaining syrup until it reaches 270 degrees, soft-crack stage.
Stream the remaining syrup mixture into the egg whites while the mixer is running. Continue to beat until the candy is thick, shiny and holds its shape. Mix in extract and nuts until fully blended and drop by spoonfuls onto greased cookie sheet. Cool until completely set.
You can pour it into a 9x9 pan, let it cool and cut into squares if you want.

Carmel-and-Chocolate-Dipped Apples

6 extra-large apples (4 pounds)
6 wooden sticks
21 ounces (about 75) vanilla caramels or chocolate caramels
3 Tbsp. water
18 ounces milk chocolate or semisweet chocolate bar, white baking bar with cocoa butter, or chocolate or vanilla-flavored candy coating, chopped
3 Tbsp. Shortening

3 cups coarsely chopped pecans, cashews, macadamia nuts, or almonds

Small multicolored decorative candies or colored sugar (optional)
6 ounces milk chocolate or semisweet chocolate bars, white baking bars with cocoa butter, or colored candy coating, chopped (optional)

1 Tbsp. shortening (optional)
6 5- to 6-inch-long candy canes (optional)

Wash and dry apples. Remove stems. Insert one wooden stick into the stem end of each apple. Set the apples aside.

In a heavy medium saucepan heat and stir the unwrapped caramels and water over medium-low heat just till caramels are melted. Dip each apple into the hot caramel mixture, spooning caramel evenly over apple. Allow excess caramel to drip off. Immediately roll apples in nuts. Place apples, bottom sides down, on waxed paper and let them stand 25 minutes or till firm.

In another heavy medium saucepan heat and stir the 18 ounces chocolate, white baking bar, or chocolate- or vanilla-flavored candy coating and the 3 tablespoons shortening over low heat just till mixture is melted. Holding apples over the saucepan, spoon the melted chocolate evenly over the caramel-and nut-coated apples. Allow excess chocolate to drip off. Place apples, bottom sides down, on waxed paper.

If desired, immediately sprinkle apples with decorative candies or colored sugar. Or, let apples stand about 1 hour till chocolate is firm. If desired, in a small saucepan heat the 6 ounces chocolate, white baking bar, or candy coating and the 1 tablespoon shortening. Then, drizzle apples with melted chocolate or colored candy coating and let stand till firm. If desired, remove wooden sticks and carefully insert candy canes into apples.

Makes 6 dipped apples

Cherry Muffins

½ cup softened sweet butter
1 cup sugar, plus extra for sprinkling atop muffins
1 tsp. Vanilla
1 egg
2 cups flour
2 tsp. Baking powder
½ tsp. Salt

½ cup milk
1 ½ cups fresh cherries, pitted and chopped, or 1 (12-ounce) package frozen cherries, defrosted and chopped
1 Tbsp. Lemon zest (optional)
½ cups pecans (optional)

Preheat oven to 375°.

Grease muffin tin (spray oil is easiest to use) or line with muffin papers.

With electric mixer, cream butter and 1 cup sugar together until light and fluffy. Beat in vanilla, then egg.

Sift 2 cups flour with baking powder and salt. Stir with milk. Fold in cherries (and lemon zest and pecans if desired.) Batter will be thick. Spoon into muffin tin, filling each cup halfway. Sprinkle tops with a little sugar.

Bake for 20 to 25 minutes or until toothpick inserted into center comes out clean. Cool for 5 minutes, then remove from pan and finish cooling on baking rack. These may be frozen.

From Harold Whiteman's collection

Chocolate No-Bake Cookies

My earliest memories of these cookies are from when I was about 5 or 6 years old. My mother used to make them for holidays and I couldn't get enough of them. Now, 53 years later, I <u>still</u> can't get enough of 'em.

1 ½ cups quick-cooking oats
½ cup flaked coconut
¼ cup chopped walnuts
¾ cup sugar

¼ cup milk
¼ cup butter
1 cup creamy peanut butter
3 Tbsp. unsweetened cocoa

In medium bowl combine oats, coconut and walnuts; set aside. In 2-quart saucepan combine sugar, milk, butter, and cocoa. Cook over medium heat, stirring occasionally, until mixture comes to a full boil, 3 to 4 minutes. Remove from heat. Stir in oats mixture and peanut butter. Quickly drop mixture by rounded teaspoonfuls onto waxed paper. Cool completely. Store in refrigerator.

Makes about 2 dozen cookies

Deep Dish Blueberry Pie

6 cups fresh blueberries or 2 (16-ounce) packages frozen blueberries, Thawed
2 Tbsp. lemon juice
1 ¼ cups sugar
3 Tbsp. quick-cooking tapioca
¼ tsp. ground cinnamon
1 Tbsp. butter, cut into 4 pieces
1 package (15 ounces) refrigerated pie crusts

Preheat oven to 400°F.

Place blueberries in large bowl and sprinkle with lemon juice.

Roll 1 crust into 12-inch circle on lightly floured work surface. Press crust into 9-inch deep-dish pie pan. Trim all but ½ inch of overhang. Spoon blueberry mixture over crust; dot top with butter pieces.

Roll remaining crust into 10-inch circle. Using small cookie cutter or knife, cut 4 or 5 shapes from crust for vents. Place crust over blueberry mixture. Trim edge, leaving 1-inch border. Fold edge under and even with pan. Crimp edge with fork.

Bake 15 minutes. Reduce heat to 350°F. Bake 40 minutes or until crust is browned and filling is bubbly. Cool on wire rack 30 minutes before serving. Makes 9 servings

Easy Coconut Cream Pie

This isn't a genuine "Ole' South" recipe, but it's really good even if it is quick and easy to make. You can add a drop or two of coconut flavoring to the mix if you want a stronger flavor.

1 ½ cups sweetened shredded coconut
2 packages (4-serving size each) vanilla pudding and pie filling mix. Plus ingredients to prepare mix
1 (6-ounce) graham cracker pie crust

Preheat oven to 350°F. Spread coconut on baking sheet. Toast coconut 10 minutes, stirring frequently; cool. Reserve 2 tablespoons coconut.

Prepare pudding according to package directions. Stir in remaining coconut.

Pour pudding mixture into pie crust. Sprinkle reserved coconut on top. Refrigerate 1 to 2 hours or until pudding is set. Makes 8 servings

Coconut Date Cookies

1 cup butter or shortening	1 tsp. baking powder
1 cup sugar	1 tsp. baking soda
1 cup brown sugar, firmly packed	1 tsp. salt
	2 cups quick-cooking oats
2 eggs	1 cup finely chopped dates
1 tsp. vanilla	1 cup broken walnuts
2 cups sifted All-purpose flour	1 cup flaked coconut

Cream together butter and sugars until light and fluffy. Add eggs, one at a time, beating well after each addition. Blend in vanilla.

Sift together flour, baking powder, baking soda and salt. Gradually add dry ingredients to creamed mixture; mix well. Stir in oats, dates, walnuts and coconut. Chill dough in refrigerator 1 hour. Drop by teaspoonfuls about 2 inches apart on greased baking sheets.

Bake in 350° oven 12 to 15 minutes or until done. Remove from baking sheets; cool on racks. Makes about 6 dozen

Coconut Macaroons

1 1/3 cups shredded coconut
1/3 cup sugar
3 Tbsp. flour

1/8 tsp. salt
2 egg whites
½ tsp. almond extract

Combine coconut, sugar, flour and slat in mixing bowl. Stir in egg whites and almond extract; mix well. Drop from teaspoon onto lightly greased baking sheets. Garnish with candied cheery halves, if desired. Bake at 325° for 20 to 25 minutes, or until edges of cookies are golden brown. Remove from baking sheets immediately.

Makes about 18

Nut Macaroons: Prepare Coconut Macaroons as directed, adding 1/3 cup chopped pecans or almonds before baking.

Chip Macaroons: Prepare Coconut Macaroons as directed, adding 1/3 cup BAKER'S® Semi-Sweet Chocolate Flavored Chips before baking.

Fruited Macaroons: Prepare Coconut Macaroons as directed, adding 1/3 cup chopped mixed candied fruit before baking. Garnish with candied cherry halves, maraschino cherries or whole almonds, if desired.

Raisin macaroons: Prepare Coconut Macaroons as directed, adding 1/3 cup raisins before baking.

Cranberry-Pecan Pie

This is another great recipe from Mr. Harold. If you like cranberries, you've got to try this!

3 eggs, slightly beaten
1 cup corn syrup, light or dark
2/3 cup sugar
2 Tbsp. Corn oil margarine, melted
1 cup fresh cranberries, coarsely chopped
1 cup pecans, coarsely chopped
1 Tbsp. Grated orange peel
1 9-inch unbaked pie shell

In medium bowl stir eggs, corn syrup, sugar and margarine until well blended. Stir in cranberries, pecans and orange peel. Pour into pie shell.

Bake in 350° oven 1 hour or until knife inserted halfway between center and edge comes out clean. Cool on rack.

From Harold Whiteman's collection of recipes

Cream Cheese Cookie Dough

1 package (8 ounces) Cream Cheese, softened
¾ cup butter, softened
1 cup powdered sugar
2 ¼ cups all-purpose flour
½ tsp. baking soda

Beat cream cheese, butter and sugar in large mixing bowl at medium speed with electric mixer until well blended. Add flour and soda; mix well.

Makes 3 cups dough

Chocolate Mint Cutouts

Heat oven to 325°F.

Add ¼ teaspoon mint extract and a few drops of green food coloring to 1 ½ cups Cookie Dough; mix well. Refrigerate 30 minutes.

On lightly floured surface, roll dough to 1/8-inch thickness; cut with assorted 3-inch cookie cutters. Place on ungreased cookie sheet.

Bake 10 to 12 minutes or until edges begin to brown. Cool on wire rack. Melt ¼ cup mint flavored semi-sweet chocolate chips in a small saucepan over low heat, stirring until smooth. Drizzle over cookies. Makes about 3 dozen cookies

Choco-Orange Slices

Heat oven to 325°F. Add 1 ½ teaspoons grated orange peel to 1 ½ cups Cookie Dough; mix well. Shape into 8x1 ½-inch log. Refrigerate 30 minutes.

Eggnog Pumpkin Pie

This is another recipe we got from one of Pauline's aunts, and it's a nice variation on the traditional pumpkin pie. The egg nog gives it a unique flavor that will liven up any holiday table.

- 1 refrigerated pie crust (half a 15 ounce package), softened as directed
- 15 ounce can pure pumpkin (not pumpkin-pie mix)
- 1 ½ cups prepared eggnog
- 2/3 cup sugar
- 1 ½ tsp. pumpkin-pie spice
- ¼ tsp. salt
- 3 large eggs
- Whipped cream, for garnish (optional)

Preheat oven to 375°F. Use pie crust dough to line a 9-inch deep dish pie pan or a 10-inch tart pan as directed on package for a 1-crust filled pie. Trim edges if necessary.

In a large bowl, with a wire whisk, mix pumpkin, eggnog, sugar, spice, salt and eggs until well blended. Place crust-lined pan on cookie sheet on oven rack; pour in pumpkin mixture (mixture will come up to almost top of pie crust).

Bake pie 55 to 65 minutes, or until filling puffs up around edges and center is just set but not puffed. Cool pie completely on wire rack. Refrigerate until ready to serve, or up to 1 day. Garnish each serving with dollops of whipped cream and sprinkle with pumpkin-pie spice (optional)

Serves 10

Holiday Cheese Ball

2 (8 ounce) packages cream cheese
1 (8 ounce) can crushed pineapple, drained
1 Tbsp. onion chopped X-fine
1 Tbsp. green bell pepper chopped X-fine
¾ tsp. seasoning salt
1 cup chopped pecans

Mix together the cream cheese, pineapple, onion, bell pepper and seasoning salt. Form into a ball and roll in topped pecans. Chill and serve with butter crackers. Makes 20 servings

Quick and Easy Cherry Pie

1 (1 lb. 8 oz.) jar cherry pie filling
¼ cup sugar
1 Tbsp. lemon juice
½ tsp. grated lemon rind
Pastry for 2-crust 8 inch pie
Butter or margarine

Combine cherry pie filling, sugar, lemon juice and lemon rind. Pour cherry pie filling into pastry-lined pie plate. Dot with butter. Adjust top crust and flute edge; cut vents.

Bake in 425° oven for 10 minutes. Reduce heat to 350° and bake for 30 minutes or until golden brown. Cool on rack.

Makes 6 to 8 servings

Butter Cookies

Cookies:
2 ½ cups all-purpose flour
1 cup granulated sugar
1 cup butter, softened
1 egg
1 tsp. baking powder
2 Tbsp. orange juice
1 Tbsp. vanilla

Frosting:
4 cups powdered sugar
½ cup butter, softened
3 to 4 Tbsp. milk
2 tsp. vanilla
Food coloring, colored sugars, flaked coconut and cinnamon candies for decorations

For cookies, in large mixing bowl combine all cookie ingredients. Beat at low speed, scraping bowl often, until well mixed, 1 to 2 minutes. If desired, divide dough into 3 equal portions; color 2/3 of dough with desired food colorings. Mix until dough is evenly colored. Wrap in plastic food wrap; refrigerate until firm, 2 to 3 hours.

Heat oven to 400°. On lightly floured surface, roll out dough, 1/3 at a time, to ¼-inch thickness. Cut out with cookie cutter.

Place 1 inch apart on ungreased cookie sheets. If desired, sprinkle colored sugars on some of the cookies or bake and decorate later. Bake for 6 to 10 minutes or until edges are lightly browned. Remove immediately. Cool completely.

For frosting, in small mixing bowl combine powdered sugar, ½ cup butter, 3 to 4 tablespoons milk and 2 teaspoons vanilla. Beat at low speed, scraping bowl often, until fluffy, 1 to 2 minutes. Frost or decorate cookies. Makes about 3 dozen (3-inch) cookies.

Fudge Walnut Brownies

½ cup butter or regular margarine
2 (1oz.) squares unsweete4ned chocolate
2 eggs
1 cup sugar
1 tsp. vanilla
¾ cups sifted All-purpose flour
½ tsp. baking powder
¼ tsp. salt
¾ cup chopped walnuts
12 Maraschino cherries(optional)

Melt butter and chocolate over low heat. Cool. Beat eggs slightly. Blend in sugar, vanilla and chocolate mixture. Stir together flour, baking powder and salt. Stir into chocolate mixture. Add walnuts. Spread in greased 11x7x1 ½ inch baking dish. Top with cherries if desired

Bake in 350° oven 30 minutes or until done. Cool in pan on rack. Cut in 2x2 inch bars. Makes about 2 dozen

Holiday Almond Balls

2 ½ cups crushed vanilla wafers
1 ¾ cups toasted ground almonds, divided
½ cup sifted powdered sugar
½ tsp. ground cinnamon
1 cup Pumpkin Pie Mix
1/3 cup almond liqueur or apple juice

In medium bowl, blend vanilla wafer crumbs, 1 cup ground almonds, powdered sugar and cinnamon. Stir in pumpkin pie mix and almond liqueur. Form into 1-inch balls. Roll in remaining ¾ cup ground almonds. Refrigerate. Makes 4 dozen.

Easy Chocolate Fudge

This isn't an "Ole South" recipe by any means, and it's not that old, but for the rush of the holidays, it's a great way to make delicious fudge that doesn't take a lot of time, and is as close to "idiot-proof" as you can get – especially if you're not a regular candy maker.

3 (6-ounce) packages semisweet chocolate chips
1 (14-ounce) can EAGLE® Brand sweetened Condensed Milk (NOT evaporated milk)
Dash salt
½ to 1 cup chopped nuts
1 ½ tsp. vanilla extract

In heavy saucepan, over low heat, melt chips with sweetened condensed milk and salt. Remove from heat; stir in nuts and vanilla. Spread evenly into wax paper-lined 8- or 9-inch square pan. Chill 2 hours or until firm. Turn fudge onto cutting board; peel off paper and cut into squares. Store loosely covered at room temperature.

Makes about 2 pounds.

Microwave: In 1-quart glass measure, combine chips with sweetened condensed milk. Microwave on high for 3 minutes. Stir until chips melt and mixture is smooth. Stir in remaining ingredients. Proceed as above.

Mexican Chocolate Fudge: Reduce vanilla to 1 teaspoon. Add 1 tablespoon ground cinnamon to sweetened condensed milk. Proceed as above.

Creamy Dark Chocolate Fudge: Melt 2 cups miniature marshmallows with chips and sweetened condensed milk. Proceed as above.

Butterscotch Fudge: Omit chocolate chips and vanilla. In heavy saucepan, melt 2 (12-ounce) packages butterscotch flavored chips with sweetened condensed milk. Remove from heat; stir in 2 tablespoons white vinegar, 1/8 teaspoon salt, ½ teaspoon maple flavoring and 1 cup chopped nuts. Proceed as above.

Creamy Milk Chocolate Fudge: Omit 1 (6-ounce) package semi-sweet chocolate chips. Add 1 cup milk chocolate chips and 2 cups miniature marshmallows. Proceed as above.

Milk Chocolate Fudge: Omit 1 (6-ounce) package semi-sweet chocolate chips. Add 1 cup milk chocolate chips. Proceed as above.

Easy Chocolate Fudge

Fresh Apple Cake

1 cup sifted flour
1 tsp. baking soda
1 tsp. ground cinnamon
1 tsp. salt
1 cup sugar
½ cup shortening

2 eggs
1 tsp. vanilla
2 ½ cups finely chopped, pared apples
1 cup chopped walnuts
1 Tbsp. flour

Sift together 1 cup flour, baking soda, cinnamon and salt.

Cream together sugar and shortening until light and fluffy. Beat in eggs, one at a time, beating well after each addition. Add vanilla. Add dry ingredients, beating well after each addition. Stir in apples. Combine walnuts and 1 tablespoon flour. Stir into batter. Pour into greased and floured 9-inch square baking pan.

Bake in 350° oven 50 minutes or until a toothpick inserted in the center comes out clean. Cool in pan on rack. Makes 9 servings

Fudge Walnut Cookies

Keep in the freezer for spur-of-the-moment entertaining.

1 ½ cup shortening
3 1/3 cup sugar
4 eggs
2 cups creamed cottage cheese
4 tsp. Vanilla
5 ½ cups sifted flour (All-purpose)
1 cup cocoa
2 tsp. Baking powder
1 tsp. Baking soda
1 tsp. Salt
1 cup chopped walnuts
1 (6 oz.) pkg. Semi-sweet chocolate pieces
Confectioners sugar

Cream together shortening and sugar until light and fluffy. Add eggs, one at a time, beating well after each addition. Blend in cottage cheese and vanilla.

Sift together flour, cocoa, baking powder, baking soda and salt. Gradually add dry ingredients to creamed mixture; mix well. Stir in walnuts and chocolate pieces. Drop by teaspoonfuls about 2 inches apart on greased baking sheets.

Bake in 350° oven 12 to 15 minutes or until done. Remove from baking sheets. Roll in confectioners sugar while still warm. Cool on racks. Makes about 11 dozen.

Ginger Nuts

1 egg white
1 tsp. cold water
1 pound lightly salted mixed nuts

½ cup sugar
1 tsp. grated lemon peel
1 tsp. grated gingerroot

In a medium mixing bowl beat the egg white with the cold water till frothy. Add the mixed nuts and stir till well combined.

In a small mixing bowl stir together the sugar, lemon peel, and gingerroot. Pour the sugar mixture over the nut mixture. Toss till the nuts are evenly coated. Spread the nuts in a single layer in a greased 15x10x1-inch baking pan.

Bake nuts in a 300° oven for 20 minutes, stirring after 10 minutes. Stir again when you remove them from the oven. Cool nuts in pan, stirring once.

To store: Prepare Ginger Nuts as directed above. Transfer nuts to a plastic bag or container. Seal, label, and place in a cool, dry place for up to 2 weeks. Makes 3 cups.

Gingersnaps

¾ cup shortening
1 cup sugar
1 egg
¼ cup molasses
2 1/4 cups sifted All-purpose flour
2 tsp. baking soda

1 tsp. salt
1 tsp. ground ginger
½ tsp. ground cinnamon
¼ tsp. ground cloves
1 ½ cup raisins
3 Tbsp. sugar

Cream together shortening and sugar until light and fluffy. Blend in egg and molasses.

Sift together flour, baking soda, salt, ginger, cinnamon and cloves. Gradually add dry ingredients to creamed mixture; mix well. Stir in raisins. Chill dough in refrigerator 8 hours or overnight.

Shape dough in 1 ¼ inch balls. Roll in 3 tablespoons sugar. Place balls about 2 inches apart on greased baking sheets.

Bake in 375° oven 12 minutes or until surface is crackled. Cool 2 minutes on baking sheets. Remove from baking sheets; cool on racks. Makes about 4 dozen.

Holiday Fruit Drops

½ cup shortening
½ cup butter or margarine
2 cups brown sugar, firmly packed
2 eggs
3 ½ sifted flour
1 tsp. baking soda

1 tsp. salt
½ cup water
1 ½ cup chopped walnuts
2 cups mixed candid fruit
½ cup halved, candied red cherries

Cream together shortening, butter and brown sugar until light and fluffy. Add eggs, one at a time, beating well after each addition.

Stir together flour, baking soda and salt. Add dry ingredients alternately with water to creamed mixture, mixing well after each addition. Stir in walnuts, candied fruit and cherries. Chill dough in refrigerator 1 hour.

Drop by teaspoonfuls on greased baking sheets.

Bake in 400° oven 8 to 10 minutes or until done. Remove from baking sheets; cool on racks. Makes 7 ½ dozen.

Holiday Fruit Salad

3 packages (3 ounces each) strawberry flavor gelatin
3 cups boiling water
2 ripe bananas
1 package (16 ounces) frozen strawberries
1 can (20 ounces) crushed pineapple in juice
1 package (8 ounces) cream cheese, softened
1 cup dairy sour cream or plain yogurt
¼ cup sugar
Crisp lettuce leaves

In large bowl, dissolve gelatin in boiling water. Slice bananas into gelatin mixture. Add frozen strawberries and untrained pineapple. Pour half the mixture into 13x9-inch pan. Refrigerate 1 hour or until firm.

In mixing bowl, beat cream cheese with sour cream and sugar; spread over chilled layer. Gently spoon remaining gelatin mixture on top. Refrigerate until firm, about 2 hours. Cut into squares; serve on lettuce-lined salad plates. Garnish with additional pineapple, if desired. Makes 12 servings.

Holiday Fruitcake

1 cup chopped candied fruit
2/3 cup pitted dates, chopped
½ cup chopped walnuts
¼ cup brandy or orange juice
1 package (6-serving size) instant pudding mix
1 package (2-layer size) yellow cake mix

4 eggs
1 cup (½ pint) sour cream
1/3 cup vegetable oil
1 Tbsp. grated orange rind
2/3 cup cold milk
Marzipan Fruits (recipe follows on next page) (optional)

MIX together candied fruit, dates, walnuts and brandy.

RESERVE 1/3 cup pudding mix; set aside. Combine cake mix, remaining pudding mix, egg, sour cream, oil and orange rind in large bowl. Beat at low speed of electric mixer just to moisten, scraping sides of bowl often. Beat at medium speed 4 minutes. Stir in fruit mixture.

POUR batter into well-greased and floured 10-inch fluted tube pan. Bake at 350° for 45 minutes or until toothpick inserted in center comes out clean. Cool in pan 15 minutes. Remove from pan; finish cooling on wire rack.

BEAT reserved pudding mix and milk in small bowl until smooth. Spoon over top of cake to glaze. Garnish with Marzipan Fruits, if desired. Makes 12 servings.

Marzipan Fruits

1 ¾ cups Coconut, finely chopped
1 package (4-serving size) gelatin, any flavor
1 cup ground blanched almonds
2/3 cup sweetened condensed milk
1 ½ tsp. sugar

1 tsp. almond extract
Food coloring (optional)
Whole cloves (optional)
Citron or angelica (optional)

MIX together coconut, dry gelatin, almonds, milk, sugar and extract. Shape by hand into small fruits, or use small candy molds. If desired, use food coloring to paint details on fruit; add whole cloves and citron for stems and blossom ends. Chill until dry. Store in covered container at room temperature up to 1 week. Makes 2 to 3 dozen confections

Marzipan Fruits

Holiday Trail Mix

1 box (8 ounces) chopped dates
1 cup whole almonds, toasted
1 cup raisins
1 cup dried banana chips
1 cup dried apricots
½ cup sunflower seed nuts

Combine all ingredients in large bowl. Holiday Trail Mix will keep up to 2 weeks in a closed container in the refrigerator. Make 12 servings

"M&M's"® Chocolate Cookies

1 cup butter or margarine, softened
1 cup packed light brown sugar
½ cup granulated sugar
2 eggs
2 tsp. vanilla
2 ¼ cups all-purpose flour
1 tsp. salt
1 tsp. baking soda
1 ½ cups "M&M's"® Plain Chocolate Candies, divided

Preheat oven to 375°F. Beat together butter, brown sugar and granulated sugar in large bowl until light and fluffy. Blend in eggs and vanilla. Combine flour, salt and baking soda in small bow. Add to butter mixture; mix well. Stir in ½ cup of the candies. Drop dough by rounded teaspoonfuls 2 inches apart onto ungreased cookie sheets. Press additional candies into top of each cookie. Bake 10 to 12 minutes or until golden brown. Remove to wire racks to cool completely. Makes about 6 dozen cookies.

Molasses Ginger Cookies

2 cups all-purpose flour
2 tsp. Baking soda
½ tsp. Salt
½ tsp. Ginger
½ tsp. Cinnamon
¼ tsp. Cloves
½ tsp. Grated orange peel

½ cup butter or margarine, softened
¼ cup vegetable shortening
1 ¼ cups sugar, divided
1 large egg
¼ cup light molasses

Heat oven to 350° F. Whisk flour, baking soda, salt, ginger, cinnamon and cloves in bowl.

Beat butter, shortening and 1 cup sugar in mixing bowl on medium speed. Beat in egg, molasses and peel until light and fluffy, 5 minutes. Reduce speed to low and add dry ingredients, just until combined.

Place remaining ¼ cup sugar in pie plate. Shape dough into 1-inch balls; roll balls in sugar (dough will be sticky). Place balls 2 inches apart on ungreased cookie sheets. Bake 10 to 12 minutes. Transfer to wire racks; cool. Makes 5 dozen

From Harold Whiteman's collection of recipes

Oatmeal Butterscotch Cookies

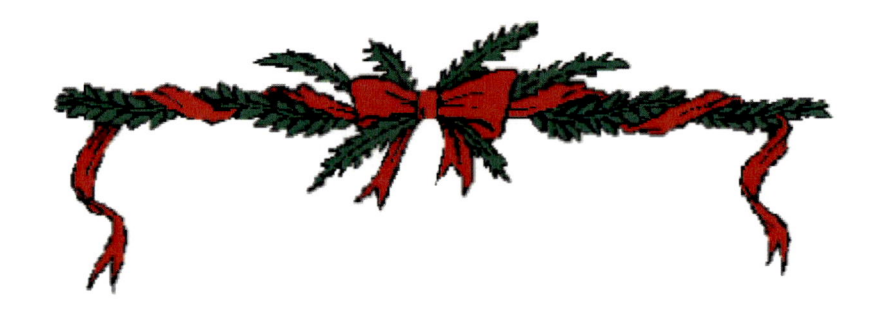

1 cup or 2 sticks of butter or margarine
¾ cup sugar
¾ cup brown sugar (firmly packed)
2 eggs

1 tsp. Vanilla extract
1 ¼ cup self-rising flour
3 cups oatmeal
12 oz. pack butterscotch chips

Bake at 375°F. For chewy cookies, bake for 7 to 8 minutes. For crispy cookies, bake for 9 to 10 minutes.

Oatmeal Date Cookies

1 cup shortening
1 cup brown sugar, firmly packed
1 cup sugar
3 eggs
1 tsp. vanilla
2 cups sifted All-purpose flour
1 tsp. baking powder
¾ tsp. baking soda
½ tsp. salt
2 cups quick-cooking oats
½ cup chopped walnuts
1 cup cut-up dates
1 cup flaked coconut

Cream together shortening and sugars until light and fluffy. Add eggs, one at a time, beating well after each addition. Blend in vanilla.

Sift together flour, baking powder, baking soda and salt. Gradually add dry ingredients to creamed mixture; mix well. Stir in oats, walnuts, dates and coconut. Drop by teaspoonfuls about 2 inches apart on greased baking sheets. Flatten with bottom of drinking glass dipped in sugar.

Bake in 375° oven 8 minutes or until lightly browned. Remove from baking sheets; cool on racks. Makes 5 dozen

Oatmeal Refrigerator Cookies

Pauline has been making this recipe she got from her mother for as long as I can remember. I'm not a big fan of oatmeal cookies, but I love these, especially on a cold morning with a hot cup of coffee.

1 cup shortening	2 Tsp. vanilla
1 cup sugar	1 ½ cup sifted All-purpose flour
1 cup brown sugar, firmly packed	1 tsp. baking soda
	½ tsp. salt
2 eggs, well beaten	3 cups quick-cooking oats

Cream together shortening and sugars until light and fluffy. Add eggs, one at a time, beating well after each addition. Blend in vanilla.

Sift together flour, baking soda and salt. Gradually add dry ingredients to creamed mixture; mix well. Stir in oats.

Divide dough in thirds. Shape into 10x1 ¼ inch rolls. Wrap tightly in plastic wrap or waxed paper. Chill several hours or overnight.

Cut rolls in thin slices. Place about 1 ½ inch apart on ungreased baking sheets.

Bake in 400° oven 6 to 8 minutes or until done. Remove from baking sheets. Cool on racks. Makes about 8 dozen.

Old-Time Gingerbread

I guess I was maybe 5 years old the first time I remember my mother making this. I can still almost smell the rich aroma while it baked. A big chunk of this stuff right out of the oven and a cold glass of milk…Mmmmm Mmmmm!

2 ½ cups sifted flour	½ cup shortening
1 ½ tsp. baking soda	½ cup sugar
1 tsp. ground ginger	1 egg
1 tsp. ground cinnamon	1 cup dark molasses
½ tsp. salt	½ cup hot water

Sift together flour, baking soda, ginger, cinnamon and salt.

Cream together shortening and sugar until light and fluffy. Add egg; beat well. Beat in molasses.

Add dry ingredients alternately with water, beating well after each addition. Pour batter into greased 9 inch square baking pan.

Bake in 350° oven 45 minutes or until cake tests done. Cool in pan on rack. Makes 9 servings.

Orange-Glazed Monkey Bread

1 cup sugar
1 tsp. grated orange zest (reserved)
1/3 cup sweetened dried cranberries
¼ cup golden raisins

3 Tbsp. orange marmalade
3 pkgs. refrigerated cinnamon rolls(12.4 oz. each)
½ cup butter
Cooking spray

Preheat oven to 350°F. Coat 12-cup Bundt pan with cooking spray.

Combine 1 cup sugar and 1 tsp. grated orange zest; reserve. Combine 1/3 cup sweetened dried cranberries, ¼ cup golden raisins and 3 Tbsp. orange marmalade.

Cut dough from 3 pkgs. (12.4 oz. each) refrigerated cinnamon rolls into quarters; reserve icing. Dip dough into ½ cup butter (melted, cooled); toss in orange sugar. Arrange 1/3 of dough in pan. Sprinkle with half of dried fruit mixture.

Repeat layering with dough, fruit mixture and dough.

Bake 35 minutes. Cool 5 minutes. Place platter over bread; invert. Remove pan and cool completely.

Combine icing and ¼ tsp. grated orange zest; drizzle on top. Garnish with cranberries, zest curls and mint. Makes 20 servings.

Peanut-Butter Cookies

When I was in elementary school, there was an older lady; Mrs. Carrie Walker, who cooked for our school. About once a week or so, she would make these cookies for dessert and I was fortunate enough to get this recipe after she retired. I reduced her recipe from enough to feed 100 kids to a normal family size. She's passed now, but her cookies live on.

1 cup all-purpose flour
1 tsp. Baking powder
1 tsp. Baking soda
½ tsp. Salt
½ cup granulated sugar
½ cup firmly packed brown sugar

¼ cup butter, softened (no substitutions)
¼ cup vegetable shortening
½ cup peanut butter
1 large egg

Heat oven to 375°F. Combine flour, baking powder, baking soda and salt in medium bowl. Set aside.

Beat sugars, butter and shortening in large mixing bowl at medium speed until light and fluffy. Beat in peanut butter and egg; beat 1 minute. Reduce speed to low; beat in flour mixture just until combined.

Press the dough into ungreased <u>deep</u> cookie sheets with a fork until just before the top of the sheet. Bake 13 to 16 minutes, until golden. DO NOT OVERBAKE (Cookies will be slightly soft but will firm up as they cool.) Cool cookies on pans 2 minutes; transfer to wire racks and cool completely then cut in about 3" squares.
Makes about 3 dozen

For variation, you can add ½ cup chocolate-coated peanut-butter candies (Reese's Pieces tm) or miniature chocolate chips. You can also use chunky peanut butter if desired.

Peanut Butter-Graham Cracker Bears

½ cup peanut butter
1/4 cup margarine or butter
1/4 cup shortening
2/3 cup granulated sugar
¼ cup packed brown sugar
¾ tsp. baking soda
1 egg

½ tsp vanilla
1 cup all-purpose flour
½ cup finely crushed graham crackers (7 cracker squares)
Miniature semisweet chocolate pieces
Frosting (optional)

Beat peanut butter, margarine or butter, and shortening in a large mixing bowl with an electric mixer on medium to high speed for 30 seconds. Add granulated sugar, brown sugar, and baking soda; beat until combined.

Beat in as much of the flour and cracker crumbs as you can with the mixer on medium speed, scraping sides of bowl occasionally. Stir in any remaining flour and crumbs with a wooden spoon.

For each bear cookie, shape some of the dough into one 1 ¼-inch ball (for body), one ¾-inch ball (for head), three balls slightly smaller than ¼-inch (for nose and ears), two 1 ½ x ½-inch logs (for arms), and two 1 ¼ x ¾-inch logs (for legs).

Note: (Flatten the balls slightly when assembling bears). Flatten the 1 ¼-inch ball for body to a 1 ¾-inch round on an ungreased cookie sheet. Attach the ¾-inch ball for the head; flatten to a 1 ¼-inch round. Attach the small balls to the head for nose and ears. Attach the 1 ½-inch logs for arms and the 1 ¼-inch logs for legs.

Decorate bears before baking by pressing in chocolate pieces, point side up, for eyes. For paws, press chocolate pieces, point side down, onto ends of arms and legs. Bake in a 325° oven for 15 to 18 minutes or until edges are lightly browned. Cool on cookie sheet 2 to 3 minutes. Remove cookies and cool on a wire rack. Add colorful frosting trims, if desired. Makes about 20 bears

Classic Cheesecake

This is the original old cheesecake recipe that's been around since I was a kid. I've been making this since I was about 12 or so, and it never gets old. It's well worth the extra trouble. It's not exactly a true "Ole' South" recipe, but it's a "gotta have" for any holiday table.

1 ½ cups Graham Cracker Crumbs	1 cup sugar
3 Tbsp. sugar	1 tsp. vanilla
1/3 cup butter or margarine, melted	4 eggs
	4 packages (8 ounces each) Cream Cheese, softened

Preheat oven to 325°F if using a silver 9-inch spring form pan (or to 300°F if using a dark nonstick spring form pan). Mix crumbs, 3 tablespoons sugar and butter; pres firmly onto bottom of pan.

Beat cream cheese, 1 cup sugar and vanilla with electric mixer on medium speed until well blended. Add eggs, 1 at a time, mixing on low speed after each addition just until blended. Pour over crust.

Bake 55 minutes or until center is almost set. Loosen cake from side of pan; cool before removing side of pan. Refrigerate 4 hours or overnight. Store leftover cheesecake in refrigerator.

Author's note:

Top with any fresh or frozen fruit just before serving. Cherry pie filling works great, too, or thawed frozen strawberries are awesome. Makes about 16 servings.

Pignoli Cookies

This is an old recipe from Mr. Harold Whiteman. These things are absolutely tongue-slappin' good if you can find the pine nuts to make them with. They're somewhat hard to find around here, but keep looking, they're well worth the effort.

1 can (12-oz.) almond paste
½ cup granulated sugar
1 cup confectioners' sugar

4 large egg whites, divided
1 ½ cups (8-oz.) pine nuts (pignoli)

Heat oven to 325° F. Line 2 cookie sheets with foil; lightly grease foil.

Blend almond paste and granulated sugar in food processor until smooth. Add confectioners' sugar and 2 egg whites; blend until smooth.

Whisk remaining 2 egg whites in small bowl until lightly beaten. Place pine nuts on large platter. With lightly floured hands, roll dough into 1-inch balls. Coat balls in egg whites, shaking off excess, then roll in pine nuts, pressing lightly to stick. Arrange balls and flatten each slightly on cookie sheets to form a 1 ½-inch round. Bake one sheet at a time, 15 to 18 minutes, until lightly browned. Let stand on cookie sheet 1 minute. Transfer to wire rack; cool.

Makes about 3 ½ dozen

From Harold Whiteman's collection of recipes

Pineapple Upside-Down Cake

Pauline found this recipe when she was in high school back in the 70's. We made it a few times at the restaurant and it always went over well. As far as I can tell it's the classic old recipe that closely resembles the one my mother had when I was a kid.

1 can (20 ounces) pineapple slices in juice	1 tsp. grated lemon peel
2/3 cup margarine	1 tsp. lemon juice
2/3 cup brown sugar, packed	1 tsp. vanilla extract
10 Maraschino cherries	1 ½ cups flour
¾ cup granulated sugar	1 ¾ tsp. baking powder
2 eggs, separated	¼ tsp. salt
	½ cup dairy sour cream

Preheat oven to 350°F. Drain pineapple; reserve 2 tablespoons liquid. In 9-or 10-inch cast iron skillet, melt 1/3 cup margarine. Remove from heat. Add brown sugar and stir until blended. Arrange pineapple slices in skillet. Place 1 cherry in center of each slice.

In large bowl, beat remaining 1/3 cup margarine with ½ cup granulated sugar until fluffy. Beat in egg yolks, lemon peel and juice, and vanilla. In medium bowl, combine flour, baking powder and salt. Blend dry ingredients into creamed mixture alternately with sour cream and reserved pineapple liquid. In large bowl, beat egg whites until soft peaks form.

Gradually beat in remaining ¼ cup granulated sugar until stiff peaks form. Fold into batter. Spread evenly over pineapple in skillet.

Bake in preheated oven about 35 minutes or until cake springs back when touched. Let stand in skillet on wire rack 10 minutes. Invert onto serving plate. Serve warm or cold. Makes 8 to 10 servings

Quilt Block Cookies

1/3 cup margarine or butter
1/3 cup shortening
2 cups all-purpose flour
¾ cup sugar
1 egg

1 Tbsp. milk
1 tsp. baking powder
1 tsp. vanilla
Egg Paint

Beat margarine and shortening with an electric mixer about 30 seconds or until softened. Add about half the flour, the sugar, egg, milk baking powder, vanilla, and dash of salt. Beat until combined. Beat or stir in remaining flour. Divide dough in half. Cover; chill about 3 hours or until easy to handle.

Roll half of the dough on a lightly floured surface to a ¼-inch thickness. Cut into 4-inch squares. Use a skewer and ruler to score quilt patterns. Use Egg Paint to color in sections. When the cookies are baked, the egg mixture becomes shiny and the score lines separate slightly, resembling the seams of a pieced quilt.

Bake in a 350° oven for 15 minutes or until done. Cool on cookie sheet 2 to 3 minutes. Remove cookies and cool on a wire rack.

Egg Paint: Beat together one egg yolk and 1 teaspoon water in a small bowl. Divide mixture among 3 or 4 small bowls. Add 2 or 3 drops of a different food coloring to each bowl; mix well. Paint on unbaked cookies with a small, clean paintbrush. If the colored mixtures thicken while standing, stir in water one drop at a time. Makes about 24 cookies.

Raisin Cookies

This is another recipe I was able to get from Mrs. Carrie Walker after she retired from the school system. I remember these cookies as if it was yesterday.

1 cup shortening
1 ½ cups sugar
3 eggs
1 tsp. vanilla
3 cups sifted plain flour
1 tsp. baking soda

¼ tsp. salt
¼ tsp. ground nutmeg
½ cup hot water
1 cup raisins or currants
1 Tbsp. flour

Cream together shortening and sugar until light and fluffy. Add eggs, one at a time, beating well after each addition. Beat in vanilla.

Sift together 3 cups flour, baking soda, salt and nutmeg. Add dry ingredients alternately with hot water to creamed mixture, mixing well after each addition.

Combine raisins and 1 tablespoon flour. Stir into dough. Drop dough by teaspoonfuls about 2 inches apart on greased baking sheets.

Bake in 400° oven 10 minutes or until golden brown. Remove from baking sheets. Cool on racks. Makes about 5 dozen

Rice Pudding

3 ½ cups milk
½ cup sugar, divided
1 cinnamon stick
½ cup long-grain rice (not parboiled or quick-cooking rice)

2 egg yolks
½ cup heavy or whipping cream
1 tsp. vanilla extract

Heat milk, ¼ cup sugar and cinnamon in saucepan just to boil; stir in rice and reduce heat to low. Cover and simmer 40 minutes.

Whisk yolks, cream, remaining ¼ cup sugar and vanilla in bowl. Stir into rice mixture. Bring to boil; cook, stirring, 2 minutes. Remove cinnamon. Cool 30 minutes. Makes 4 servings

From Harold Whiteman's collection of recipes

Skillet Gingerbread

2 eggs
¾ cup brown sugar, packed well
¾ cup melted shortening (not butter)
2 ½ cups plain flour
1 ¾ tsp. soda

2 ½ tsp. ground ginger
1/2 tsp. baking powder
1 cup boiling water
¾ cup country molasses
1 ½ tsp. cinnamon
½ tsp. cloves
½ tsp. nutmeg

Add well-beaten eggs to the sugar, molasses and melted shortening. Then add the flour, which has been sifted with spices, soda and baking powder. Beat well, and lastly add the boiling water, BEAT. Pour into a heavy, round well-greased skillet. Bake at 325° for 30 to 40 minutes. Test for doneness at 30 minutes; in the long ago, a straw from a straw broom would be used; if it came out clean the bread was done.

From Harold Whiteman's collection.

Sue's Apple Butter Spice Cake

This is an awesome recipe from our friend and neighbor, Mary Sue Gregg who graciously offered us a few recipes for our books. I had a taste of this cake last Christmas, and it surely deserves a spot on the dessert table.

Topping:

½ cup brown sugar (firmly packed)
1 tsp. Cinnamon
½ tsp. Nutmeg
½ cup chopped walnuts (Pecans can be substituted)

Combine above ingredients and set aside.

Cake:

2 cups sifted flour
1 tsp. Baking powder
1 tsp. Baking soda
½ tsp. Salt
½ cup butter or margarine
1 cup sugar
2 eggs (medium or large)
¾ cup of Apple Butter (Not Apple Sauce)
1 tsp. Vanilla
½ cup All Bran Cereal
1 cup sour cream

Preheat oven to 350°.
In medium size bowl, sift together flour, baking powder, soda, and salt. Blend in the butter and sugar. Add the eggs and beat well. Stir in the Apple Butter, Vanilla and All Bran. Add sour cream and blend well.

Pour half the batter into a greased 13x9-inch baking pan. Spread half the topping over batter. Gently spread remainder of batter over the topping and then spread the rest of the topping on the top.

Bake at 350° for about 40 to 45 minutes. Can be served hot or cold. I use a dash of whipped cream on top.

"Mama Sue" Gregg

Sue's Coconut Custard Pie

I dearly love custard of any kind, and I was overjoyed when "Mama Sue" gave us this recipe. I haven't had the time to make it myself yet, but I had some last year, and I pray she makes it again this year!

4 eggs
½ cup sugar
¼ tsp. salt
2 1/3 cups milk

2 tsp. vanilla
¾ cup shredded coconut
nutmeg

Beat eggs lightly with fork. Add sugar, salt, milk, vanilla and coconut. Whip slightly. Pour into unbaked shell. Sprinkle with nutmeg. Bake at 425° for 40 minutes or until knife inserted in center of pie comes out clean.

"Mama Sue" Gregg

Buttermilk Chocolate Chip Cookies

1 cup shortening
1 cup sugar
1 cup brown sugar, firmly packed
2 eggs
1 ½ tsp. vanilla

3 cups sifted All-purpose flour
1 tsp. baking soda
½ cup buttermilk
1 (6oz.) pkg. semi-sweet chocolate pieces
1 cup chopped walnuts

Cream together shortening and sugars until light and fluffy. Beat in eggs one at a time. Blend in vanilla. Sift together flour and baking soda. Add dry ingredients alternately with buttermilk to creamed mixture; mix well. Stir in chocolate pieces and walnuts. Drop by teaspoonfuls about 2 inches apart on greased baking sheet. Bake in 350° oven 12 to 15 minutes or until done. Remove from baking sheets; cool on racks. Makes 7 dozen

Sweet Potato Bread

15- to 16-ounce package nut quick bread mix
2 tsp. ground cinnamon
¼ tsp. ground nutmeg
¼ tsp. ground ginger or 1/8 tsp. Ground cloves
1 cup water
1 beaten egg

½ cup drained and mashed canned sweet potatoes or canned pumpkin
2 Tbsp. cooking oil
Orange Icing (optional) or Cream Cheese Frosting (optional)

Grease and lightly flour one 8x4x2-inch loaf pan or five 4 ½ x 2 2 ½-inch loaf pans. Set the pans aside.

Stir together the quick bread mix, cinnamon, nutmeg, and ginger or cloves in a large mixing bowl. Add water, sweet potato or pumpkin, egg, and oil. Stir just until dry ingredients are moistened.

Pour the batter into prepared pan(s). bake in a 350° oven until a toothpick inserted near the center(s) comes out clean. Allow 60 to 65 minutes baking time for large pan or 30 to 35 minutes baking time for small pans.

Cool in pan(s) on a wire rack for 10 minutes. Remove from pans; cool completely on rack. If desired, wrap in clear plastic wrap and store loaves overnight in a cool, dry place for easier slicing. If desired, drizzle loaves with orange icing or cream cheese frosting before serving or giving. Makes 1 large loaf or 5 small loaves.

Orange Icing: in a small mixing bowl stir together 1 cup unsifted powdered sugar and enough orange juice to make of drizzling consistency (about 1 tablespoon).

Sue's Monkey Bread

This delicious Monkey Bread recipe from "Mama Sue" is a favorite at our neighborhood gatherings every Christmas. It's made the old way from scratch with flour and yeast, allowed to rise on the cutting board. It's well worth the little extra trouble.

Bread:
2 (14 oz.) Packages active dry yeast
2 cups hot tap water
1 tsp. Sugar
1 Tbs. Ft margarine
1 ½ tsp. Salt
Flour, as needed

Dip:
1 cup melted margarine
½ tsp. Garlic powder
½ tsp. Dried Italian spices
½ tsp. Celery salt

In a large bowl, stir yeast, sugar, and water together. Let rest for about 5 to 10 minutes, until it foams. Stir in 1 cup of flour and the soft margarine. Stir to a sticky dough. (You can use a mixer at this stage on slow speed.) Add about 1 ½ to 2 cups flour with spoon to make a stiff dough.

Turn out onto floured board. Let rest 5 minutes. (I usually wash bowl and lightly grease it plus make my dip at this time.) Turn dough over to flour on each side. Knead and turn dough about 10 times. Return dough to greased bowl, turning once to have grease on both sides. Cover with cloth. Let rise in warm place until doubled.

[Dip is made by heating 1 cup margarine in small pan or microwave dish. Add other spices and set aside.] Any extra left over can be used as a spread for bread.

Once the dough has doubled, return to floured board. Knead in a small amount of flour to keep it from sticking to fingers. Flatten dough to an inch thick, (Doesn't matter what the shape), and cut into 1 ½ inch strips. Cut strips into small pieces about the size of a walnut. Here I use a bunt pan but any baking size will do. You can make hamburger buns or cloverleaf rolls at this time, too. Dip pieces into cooled margarine mixture, getting all sides coated. Be sure to push them against each other.

Bake at 375° for 25 to 30 minutes in bunt pan, 35 to 45 minutes for hamburger buns, or 20 to 30 minutes for cloverleaf rolls. They are done if they sound hollow when tapped on top.

Hope you enjoy this recipe. I've been using it since 1950 when my Mother taught it to me.

"Mama Sue" Gregg

Sugar Cookies

This is a recipe I found in one of my mother's cookbooks which was old when I was a kid. It's at least 58 years old that I know of.

1 cup butter or margarine	1 tsp. vanilla
1 cup sugar	4 cups sifted flour
1 cup sifted confectioners sugar	1 tsp. baking soda
2 eggs	1 tsp. cream of tartar
1 cup shortening (melted)	½ tsp. salt

Cream together butter and sugars until it fluffs up. Add eggs, one at a time, beating well after each one. Blend in melted shortening and vanilla.

Sift together flour, baking soda, cream of tartar and salt. Gradually add dry ingredients to creamed mixture; mix well. Chill dough in refrigerator 8 hours or overnight.

Shape dough in balls the size of a walnut. Place balls about 2 inches apart on ungreased baking sheets or roll dough out and cut shapes using cookie cutters.

Bake in 350° oven 10 to 12 minutes or until done. Remove from baking sheets; cool on racks. Makes about 7 dozen.

Cream Cheese Frosting:

16-ounce package cream cheese, softened
1 cup confectioner's sugar
3 ½ Tbsp. heavy cream

2 Tbsp. grated orange rind
1 tsp. cinnamon
2 tsp. Vanilla

Whip cream cheese, slowly adding sugar, until fluffy. Add heavy cream, orange rind, cinnamon and vanilla. Mix well. Makes about 2 ¼ cups.

Cream Cheese Frosting from Harold Whiteman's collection of recipes.

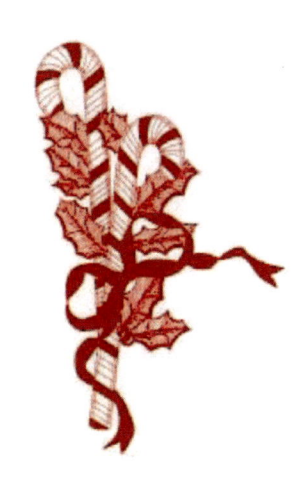

White Coconut Cake

This is another cake recipe from my childhood. This was my mother's favorite cake and usually the one she made the most. If you like coconut cake, this is a great one.

2 ¼ cups sifted cake flour	1 cup ice water
2 ¼ tsp. baking powder	4 egg whites
¼ tsp. salt	½ cup sugar
½ cup shortening	½ cup flaked coconut
1 cup sugar	

Sift together cake flour, baking powder and salt. Cream together shortening and 1 cup sugar until light and fluffy. Beat in vanilla.

Add dry ingredients alternately with ice water, beating well after each addition.

Beat egg whites until foamy. Gradually add ½ cup sugar, beating until stiff peaks form. Fold into batter. Pour batter into 2 8 inch round cake pans.

Bake in 350° oven 30 minutes or until cakes test done. Cool in pans on racks 10 minutes. Remove from pans; cool on racks.

Prepare your favorite fluffy white frosting. Frost cake and garnish with flaked coconut. Makes 12 servings.

Buttery Peanut Brittle

This has been a holiday favorite for as many years as I can remember. I found this in one of my Mother's old cookbooks years ago. It makes a great gift when you pack it up in one of those Christmasy tins.

2 Cups sugar	1 cup butter, cut into pieces
1 cup light corn syrup	2 cups raw Spanish peanuts
½ cup water	1 tsp. baking soda

In 3-puart saucepan combine sugar, corn syrup and water. Cook over low heat, stirring occasionally, until sugar is dissolved and mixture come to a full boil, 20 to 30 minutes.

Add butter; continue cooking, stirring occasionally, until candy thermometer reaches 280°F or small amount of mixture dropped into ice water forms a pliable strand, 80 to 90 minutes.

Stir in peanuts; continue cooking, stirring constantly, until candy thermometer reaches 305°F or small amount of mixture dropped into ice water forms a brittle strand, 12 to 14 minutes.

Remove from heat; stir in baking soda. Pour mixture onto 2 buttered cookie sheets; spread about ¼ inch thick.

Cool completely; break into pieces. Makes 2 pounds

Classic Crisco® Pie Crust

8-, 9- or 10-inch Single Crust

1 1/3 cups all-purpose flour
½ tsp. salt

½ cup CRISCO® Shortening
3 Tbsp. cold water

8- or 9-inch Double Crust

2 cups all-purpose flour
1 tsp. salt

¾ cup CRISCO® Shortening
5 Tbsp. cold water

10-inch Double Crust

2 2/3 cups all-purpose flour
1 tsp. salt

1 cup CRISCO® Shortening
7 to 8 Tbsp. cold water

For pie dough, spoon flour into measuring cup and level. Combine flour and salt in medium bowl. Cut in Crisco® using pastry blender (or 2 knives) until all flour is blended to form pea-size chunks. Sprinkle with water, 1 tablespoon at a time. Toss lightly with fork until dough will form a ball.

For single crust, press dough between hands to form 5- to 6- inch "pancake." Flour lightly on both sides. Roll between sheets of waxed paper on dampened countertop until 1 inch larger than upside-down pie plate. Peel off top sheet. Flip into pie plate. Remove other sheet. Fold dough edge under and flute.
For recipes using a **baked** pie crust, heat oven to 425°F. Prick bottom and side thoroughly with fork (50 times) to prevent shrinkage. Bake 10 to 15 minutes or until lightly browned. (For recipes using an **unbaked** pie crust, follow baking directions given in that recipe.)

For double crust, divide dough in half. Roll each halt separately as described in step 2. Transfer bottom crust to pie plate. Trim edge even with pie plate. Add desired filling to unbaked pie crust. Moisten pastry edge with water. Lift top crust onto filled pie. Trim ½-inch beyond edge of pie plate. Fold top edge under bottom crust. Flute. Cut slits in top crust to allow steam to escape. Bake according to specific recipe directions.

Whole Wheat Pie Shell

1 cup whole wheat flour
¼ tsp. Salt

¼ cup vegetable oil
3 Tbsp. Ice water

Preheat oven to 375°

Combine flour and salt in a medium-size mixing bowl; make a well in center. Add oil and water; mix lightly with a fork until pastry holds together and leaves sides of bowl clean.

Roll out to an 11-inch round between two pieces of waxed paper; fit into a 9-inch pie plate. Flute to make a stand-up edge. Prick shell all over with a fork.

Press and shape dough into pan; prick bottom with a fork.

Bake in a hot oven (425°) for 15 minutes, or until pastry is lightly browned. Cool.

From Harold Whiteman's collection of recipes

Candy-Filled Wagon Cake

1 (13x9x2-inch) oblong cake
Creamy Butter Frosting (page 137)
Yellow food color
Creamy Chocolate Icing (page 137)
Assorted candies and animal cookies
1 large gingerbread man
Red licorice string

Place cake on large tray or platter.

Tint Creamy Butter Frosting bright yellow. Frost sides and top of cake.

Using tip 21 with Creamy Chocolate Icing, pipe a border around top edge of cake to form sides of wagon. Also pipe another border around bottom of edge of cake.

Pipe *Happy Holidays or Merry Christmas* using tip 2 on 2/3 of cake. Arrange assorted candies and animal cookies on remaining 1/3 of cake. Animal cookies can be placed in frosting around sides of wagon, if you wish.

Place gingerbread man in front of wagon. Attach red licorice string to front of wagon and put in hand of gingerbread man. Makes 16 servings.

Creamy Butter Frosting

1/3 cup soft butter or regular margarine
1 (1 lb.) pkg. Confectioners sugar
5 Tbsp. evaporated milk
1/8 tsp. Salt
1 tsp. Almond extract

Cream butter until soft and smooth. Gradually add confectioners sugar alternately with the evaporated milk, Beating well after each addition. Add salt and almond extract, beating until smooth and creamy. Makes 2 cups

---

Creamy Chocolate Icing

This delicious frosting can be used for any cake.
½ cup soft butter or regular margarine
1 (1 lb.) pkg. confectioners sugar
2 (1 oz.) squares unsweetened chocolate, melted
2 Tbsp. evaporated milk
¼ tsp. salt
1 tsp. vanilla

Cream butter until soft and smooth. Gradually add confectioners sugar, beating well after each addition. Stir n melted chocolate, evaporated milk, salt and vanilla. Mix until smooth and creamy. Makes 2 ½ cups

Easy Carrot Cake

1 ¼ cups MIRACLE WHIP® Salad Dressing
1 package (2-layer size) yellow cake mix
4 eggs
¼ cup cold water
2 tsp. ground cinnamon
2 cups finely shredded carrots
½ cup chopped walnuts
1 container (16 ounces) ready-to-spread cream cheese frosting

Heat oven to 350°F.

Beat salad dressing, cake mix, eggs, water and cinnamon at medium speed with electric mixer until well blended. Stir in carrots and walnuts. Pour into greased 13x9-inch baking pan.

Bake 30 to 35 minutes or until wooden pick inserted in center comes out clean. Cool completely. Spread cake with frosting. Makes 12 servings.

Easy Peanut Butter Cookies

1 (14-ounce) can EAGLE® Brand Sweetened Condensed Milk (NOT evaporated milk)
¾ cup smooth peanut butter
2 Cups biscuit baking mix
1 tsp. vanilla extract
Granulated sugar

Preheat oven to 375°. In large mixer bowl, beat sweetened condensed milk and peanut butter until smooth. Add biscuit mix and vanilla; mix well. Shape into 1-ince balls. Roll in sugar. Place 2 inches apart on ungreased baking sheets. Flatten with fork. Bake 6 to 8 minutes or until lightly browned (do not overbake). Cool. Store tightly covered at room temperature. Makes about 5 dozen.

Peanut Blossoms: Shape as above; do not flatten. Bake as above. Press solid milk chocolate candy in center of each ball immediately after baking.

Peanut Butter and Jelly Gems: Press thumb in center of each ball of dough; fill with jelly, jam or preserves. Bake as above.

Any-Way-You-Like'm Cookies: Stir 1 cup semi-sweet chocolate chips or chopped peanuts or raisins or flaked coconut into dough. Proceed as above.

Shortcut Cappuccino Caramels

1 cup margarine or butter
1 (16-ounce package) 2 ¼ cups packed brown sugar
1 (14-ounce can) 1 ¼ cups sweetened condensed milk (not evaporated milk)
1 cup light corn syrup
3 Tbsp. instant coffee crystals
1 cup chopped walnuts
1 tsp. vanilla
½ to 1 tsp. finely shredded orange peel
64 or 81 small walnut halves or chocolate-covered coffee bean candies (optional)

Line an 8x8x2-inch or a 9x9x2-inch baking pan with foil, extending foil over edges of pan. Butter the foil; set pan aside. In a heavy 3-quart saucepan melt the margarine or butter over low heat. Stir in the brown sugar, sweetened condensed milk, corn syrup, and coffee crystals. Carefully clip a candy thermometer to the side of the saucepan.

Cook over medium heat, stirring frequently, till the thermometer register 248° or candy reaches firm-ball stage*. Mixture should boil at a moderate, steady rate over the entire surface. Reaching firm-ball stage should take 15 to 20 minutes.

Remove the saucepan from the heat. Remove the candy thermometer from the saucepan. Immediately stir in the 1 cup chopped walnuts, vanilla, and orange peel. Quickly pour the caramel mixture into the prepared baking pan. If desired, place walnut halves or chocolate coffee beans 1 inch apart on top of caramel. Press the walnut halves or chocolate coffee beans slightly onto the caramel.

When caramel is firm, use foil to lift it out of the pan. Use a buttered knife to cut the caramel into squares, cutting between the walnut halves or chocolate coffee beans. Wrap each caramel piece in confectioners' foil or in clear plastic wrap.

*To test the candy for firm-ball stage, drop a few drops of the caramel mixture into a custard cup of *very cold water*. Shape the drops of the caramel mixture into a ball. When the caramel ball is removed from the water, it will be firm enough to hold its shape, but should quickly flatten at room temperature. Makes 64 or 81 pieces or about 3 pounds

To store: Prepare and wrap Shortcut Cappuccino Caramels as directed above. Place caramels in a freezer container. Seal, label, and freeze for up to 9 months. Thaw, covered, at room temperature about 1 hour before packaging.

To Family and good friends, may you be safe and happy all through the holiday season and the coming New Year!

DRINKS

Apple-Berry Cider

8 cups apple cider or apple juice
1 (10-ounce) package frozen red raspberries or frozen sliced strawberries
4 inches stick cinnamon
1 ½ tsp. whole cloves
1 large apple (optional)
Cinnamon sticks (optional)

Combine apple cider or juice, frozen raspberries or strawberries, cinnamon, and cloves in a large saucepan. Bring to boiling; reduce heat. Cover and simmer for 10 minutes. Strain through a sieve lined with 100% cotton cheesecloth.

To serve, pour warm cider into 8 heat-proof glasses or cups. If desired, cut 1/8-inch-thick slices from apple, then cut stars or other holiday shapes freehand or using canape cutters. Float a shape in each mug of cider and garnish with a cinnamon stick. Makes 8 (8-ounce) servings.

Cranberry Wassail

1 (32-ounce) jar cranberry juice cocktail
1 cup water
½ of a 6-ounce can (1/3 cup) frozen pineapple-orange juice concentrate, thawed
6 inches stick cinnamon
2 whole cloves
Orange peel strips (optional)
Stick cinnamon (optional)

In a large saucepan stir together the cranberry juice cocktail, water, pineapple-orange juice concentrate, the 6 inches stick cinnamon, and cloves. Bring to boiling; reduce heat. Cover and simmer for 10 minutes.

Using a slotted spoon, remove cinnamon and cloves from juice mixture. Transfer the juice mixture to a container. Cool slightly. Cover and refrigerate for up to 7 days.

To reheat the juice mixture, transfer it to a large saucepan and heat till warm. Carefully pour into a heatproof punch bowl. Ladle juice into cups and, if desired, garnish with orange peel strips tied around stick cinnamon.   Makes 10 (4 ½-ounce) servings.

Ginger Tea

Note: Ginger helps clear congestion and soothe sore throats.

1 ½ cups water
2 tsp. sugar

1 tsp. Peeled, grated fresh ginger
1 tsp. Grated orange peel

Combine the above ingredients in a small saucepan. Bring to a boil; reduce heat to low and simmer 10 minutes. Strain tea through fine sieve into 12-ounce mug. Makes 1 serving.

From Harold Whiteman's collection of recipes

Chocolate-Peppermint Martini

1 cup half-and-half
¼ cup vodka

¼ cup chocolate syrup
2 tsp. peppermint schnapps

If desired, dip rims of 2 martini glasses in water, then into red decorating sugar. In large cocktail shaker, combine 1 cup half-and-half, ¼ cup vodka, ¼ cup chocolate syrup and 2 tsp. peppermint schnapps; add ice. Cover; shake 30 seconds. Strain into glasses. If desired, garnish with whipped cream or topping, chocolate shavings and mini candy canes. Makes 2 servings.

Cranberry Margarita

In a large pitcher, stir together 3 cups cranberry juice, 1 can (12 ounces) frozen limeade concentrate (thawed), 1 cup tequila and 3 Tbsp. triple sec; refrigerate until chilled, at least 1 hour. If desired, dip rims of 8 margarita glasses in water, then into light green decorating sugar. If desired, serve over ice garnished with skewered lime slices and fresh cranberries. Makes 8 servings.

No-alcohol version: Replace tequila and triple sec with orange juice.

Christmas Carol Punch

2 medium red apples
2 quarts clear apple cider
8 cinnamon sticks
2 tsp. whole cloves

½ cup raisins
Orange slices
Lemon slices
¼ cup lemon juice

Core apples; slice into ½-inch rings. In Dutch oven, combine cider, cinnamon, cloves, apple rings and raisins. Bring to boil over high heat; reduce heat to low and simmer 5 to 8 minutes or until apples are just tender. Remove cloves; add orange and lemon slices and lemon juice. Pour into punch bowl. Ladle into large mugs, including an apple ring, some raisins and citrus slices in each serving. Serve with spoons. Makes about 2 quarts.

Santa's Cocoa Mix

- 1 8-quart package (about 10 cups) nonfat dry milk powder
- 1 16-ounce package (about 4 ¾ cups) sifted powdered sugar
- 1 ¾ cups unsweetened cocoa powder
- 1 ½ instant malted milk powder
- 1 6-ounce jar (1 ¾ cups) powdered nondairy creamer
- Marshmallows or whipped cream (optional)

Combine nonfat dry milk powder, powdered sugar, unsweetened cocoa powder, instant malted milk powder, and nondairy creamer in a large bowl. Stir until thoroughly combined. Store cocoa mixture in an airtight container.

For each individual serving, place 1/3 cup cocoa mixture in a mug; add ¾ cup boiling water. Stir to dissolve. Top with marshmallows or a dollop of whipped cream. Makes enough for about 48 (8-ounce) servings.

Blu-Tini

In a pitcher, stir together 2 Tbs Blue Curacao, 1 Tbs Tequila, 1 Tbs White Rum, and 1 Tbs vodka. Add 1 cup lemon-lime soda. Serve over ice. Garnish with lime wedges and lemon zest. Makes 2 servings.

Mulled Wine

Using vegetable peeler, remove the zest of one orange in thin strips. In a large pot, combine 1 bottle (750ml) Merlot wine, ½ cup sugar, 2 cinnamon sticks, 1 tsp vanilla extract, 4 peppercorns and the orange zest strips. Heat over low heat until just warm – about 8-10 minutes. Do not boil. Garnish with cinnamon sticks and clove-studded orange slices. Makes 4 servings.

Blushing Pear Prosecco Cocktail

In a small pitcher, combine ½ cup pear nectar (chilled), 2 tsp grenadine syrup, and ¾ cup Prosecco wine (chilled). Divide between 2 glasses. Garnish with pear slices. For a no-alcohol version, substitute the wine for ginger ale. Makes 2 servings.

Christmas Jones

4 fresh strawberries
 1 part vodka
 2 tsp superfine sugar

5 oz pineapple juice
 7-Up
 mint sprigs for garnish

In a blender, whiz the vodka, strawberries, sugar and pineapple juice together. Pour the mix equally into two highball glasses. Top with 7-Up. Garnish with a sprig of mint.

Coquito

Coquito is Traditional Puerto Rican Eggnog made with coconut milk. Try it, it is delicious!

½ tsp. cinnamon
pinch of salt
½ cup water
1 cup Rum
14 oz condensed milk

15 oz can of cream of coconut
30 oz coconut milk
4 eggs
sugar to taste

Combine all ingredients and mix well with an electric mixer or blender. Store in the refrigerator. Serve in small glass cups. Enjoy!

Traditional Eggnog

2 cups heavy cream, lightly whipped
1/2 cup Rum
3/4 cup Brandy

12 egg whites
3/4 cup rye Whiskey
1 cup sugar
12 egg yolks

Beat egg yolks and add half of the sugar and all of the alcohol. Beat egg whites until stiff and add remaining sugar to them. Add the two mixtures together and fold in the lightly whipped cream. Garnish with grated nutmeg. Enjoy! Serves 30.

Non-alcoholic Eggnog

1 quart (2%) milk
6 eggs
1/4 teaspoon salt
1/2 cup sugar

1 teaspoon vanilla or rum extract
1 cup whipping cream
ground nutmeg

Place milk in a 2 quart measuring cup. Heat on high in microwave for 4 to 6 minutes or until hot. (Do not boil).

Beat together eggs and salt in large bowl. Gradually beat in the sugar. Slowly pour the hot milk mixture into the eggs while continuing to beat.

Pour back into the 2 quart glass measuring cup. Heat on high two to three minutes. Remove from microwave and insert thermometer into mixture. It should register 160°F. Stir in vanilla or rum extract.

Cool by setting the bowl in very cold water. Stir for 10 minutes.

Cover and refrigerate until thoroughly chilled, several hours or overnight. Pour into punch bowl or pitcher. Fold in whipped cream and dust with nutmeg. Makes 2 quarts.

Traditional Fruit Punch

This Fruit Punch Recipe is made with pineapple juice, strawberries, ice cream, and lemon lime soda.

1 (12-ounce) can frozen pineapple juice concentrate, thawed
2 (10-ounces each) package frozen strawberries, thawed

2 pints strawberry ice cream
2 liter bottle chilled lemon-lime soda (Sprite ^{tm} or 7 UP ^{tm})

Combine pineapple juice concentrate, strawberries, and 1 pint of ice cream; blend until smooth. To serve, pour into chilled punch bowl and add chilled lemon lime soda. Spoon remaining ice cream on top. Serve in punch cups.

A New Years Prayer

Photo and Poem By: Pauline Worthington

Here is a little prayer from me for you; may all of your wishes and dreams come true; for a wonderful life, world peace, true love, abundance and good health for you, your family, and the ones that you love!!!

May all of your darkness turn into light as the beautiful white flower brightens the darkest of nights!

May you have all of the passion and romance that your heart desires, may your love life set your soul on fire!

May your days nor nights never be lonely, sad, or blue and may the coming new year be prosperous for you!

May your life be filled with so much joy and happiness too; that depression can never creep up on you!

Much love to all, from me to you; please be careful in all that you do, so the new year may be accident free, and be the very best year that it can possibly be!

I pray God's angel's, forever watch over you; while guiding you in all that you choose to pursue, or with whatever life should ever bring to you and your loved ones too!

May all of your fantasies be fulfilled as the New Year approaches with great appeal!

So; good bye to the old and on with the new, may the coming new year be GREAT for you!

Happy New Year!

ABOUT THE AUTHORS,

Michael and Pauline Worthington have both been cooking since before they were teens. Michael grew up on a small farm in Tennessee and Pauline was pretty much a city girl from Hattiesburg, MS up until 1997 when she and Michael moved to the countryside of Lumberton, Mississippi where they still live now.

They owned and operated the Canopy Club Café for almost three years at the airport in Lumberton, serving food and drinks to the skydivers who come out on weekends to jump. They also served folks in town through the week with hot lunches and sandwiches as well as salads and fresh seafood in season.

During the time they ran the café, they developed several variations of old time recipes that were a huge success. Due to health considerations, and the economy, they sold the café in the Spring of 2011 and now just cook for the sheer pleasure of making a delicious meal, and write about it in their cookbooks.

Index

Apple-Berry Cider – 132
Aunt Pansy's Carrot Cake – 60
Aunt Pansy's Chicken and Dumplings – 52
Autumn Casserole – 49
Autumn Edible Centerpiece – 3
Baby Lima Beans w/ Onions – 41
Bacon and Egg Potato Salad – 42
Bacon and Mushroom Rollups – 11
Bacon Mini Croissants – 20
BBQ Chicken w/Homemade BBQ sauce – 35
Blu-Tini – 136
Blushing Pear Prosecco Cocktail – 137
Butter Cookies – 84
Buttermilk Chocolate Chip Cookies – 114
Buttery Peanut Brittle – 121
Buttery Pecan Caramels – 70
Cajun-Baked Oysters – 12
Cajun Chicken Nuggets – 16
Candied Sweet Potatoes – 43
Candy-Filled Wagon Cake – 124
Candy Bar Sleds – 6
Candy Race Cars – 4
Canopy Club Squash Casserole – 50
Caramel and Chocolate-Dipped Apples – 72
Carrot Raisin Salad – 46
Cheese and Cold Cuts Tray w/Ranch Dip – 8
Cheese Stuffed Tomatoes – 14
Cheesy Potato Skins – 15
Cherry Muffins – 74
Choco-Orange Slices – 81
Chocolate-Peppermint Martini – 134
Chocolate Mint Cutouts – 81
Chocolate No-Bake Cookies – 75
Christmas Carol Punch – 135
Christmas Jones - 137

Citrus and Herb Turkey – 32
Classic Apple Pie – 64
Classic Cheesecake – 105
Classic Crisco Pie Crust – 122
Coconut Date Cookies – 78
Coconut Macaroons – 79
Coquito – 138
Crabmeat Appetizers – 15
Cranberry Candy – 71
Cranberry Pecan Pie – 80
Cranberry Cobbler – 65
Cranberry Margarita – 135
Cranberry Wassail – 133
Cream Cheese Cookie Dough – 81
Cream Cheese Frosting – 119
Creamy Butter Frosting – 125
Creamy Chocolate Icing – 125
Creamy Corn Pudding – 44
Crispy Fried Mushrooms – 19
Deep Dish Blueberry Pie – 76
Deep Fried Turkey – 28
Devilish Deviled Eggs – 13
Easy Carrot Cake – 126
Easy Chocolate Fudge – 86
Easy Coconut Cream Pie – 77
Easy Peanut Butter Cookies – 127
Easy Rocky Road Bars – 67
Eggnog Pumpkin Pie – 82
Fresh Apple Cake – 88
Fudge Walnut Brownies – 85
Fudge Walnut Cookies – 89
Ginger Nuts – 90
Ginger Tea – 134
gingersnaps – 91
Glazed baby Carrots – 47
Glazed Baked Ham – 25
Green Bean, New Potato, and Ham Salad – 48
Herb-Parmesan Bread – 68
Herb-Roasted Turkey - 30, , Holiday Almond Balls – 85

Holiday Baked Ham – 24
Holiday Carrot Dip – 7
Holiday Cheese Ball – 83
Holiday Fruit Drops – 92
Holiday Fruit Salad – 93
Holiday Fruitcake – 94
Holiday Ham Logs – 10
Holiday Trail Mix – 96
Honey-Date Pumpkin Cookies – 66
Horseradish Sauce – 11
Jambalaya – 36
M+M's Chocolate Cookies – 96
Mama's Chicken and Dumplings – 34
Mama's Cornbread Dressing – 56
Mama's Pumpkin Pie – 61
Marzipan Fruits – 95
Molasses Ginger Cookies – 97
Mulled Wine – 137
New Orleans Stuffed Shrimp – 9
Non-Alcoholic Eggnog – 139
Oatmeal Butterscotch Cookies – 98
Oatmeal Date Cookies – 99
Oatmeal Refrigerator Cookies – 100
Old-Time Gingerbread – 101
Orange-Glazed Monkey Bread – 102
Patricia's Divine Divinity – 71
Pauline's Holiday Dressing – 54
Peanut Butter-Graham Cracker Bears – 104
Peanut Butter Cookies 103
Pignoli Cookies – 106
Pineapple Upside-Down Cake – 107
Pork Chops w/ Rice and Gravy – 38
Quick and Easy Cherry Pie – 83
Quick and Easy Pecan Pie – 63
Quilt Block Cookies – 108
Raisin Cookies – 109
Real Whipped Cream – 62
Red Beans and Rice – 5
Rice Pudding – 110

Santa's Cocoa Mix – 136
Sausage and Grape Stuffing – 33
Sausage Party Rolls – 17
Scandinavian Party Tray – 18
Shortcut Cappaccino Caramels – 128
Skillet Gingerbread – 111
Southwest Meatballs – 18
Spinach Dip w/Hawaiian Bread – 21
Stuffed Acorn Squash – 45
Stuffed Mushrooms – 13
Sue's Apple Butter Spice Cake – 112
Sue's Coconut Custard Pie – 113
Sue's Monkey Bread – 116
Sugar Cookies – 118
Sugared Fruit Edible Centerpiece – 5
Sweet Potato Bread – 115
Taco Snack Mix – 19
Teriyaki Mini-Kabobs – 14
The Best Roast Turkey Ever – 26
Traditional Eggnog – 138
Traditional Fruit Punch – 140
Tropical Cheese Dip – 7
Vegetable Tray w/ Ranch Dip – 8
White Coconut Cake – 120
Whole Wheat Pie Shell - 123, ,

Boys and Their Toys!

These are our 3 Grandsons at Christmas. Left to right: Michael Allen Smith, Jiles Allrick Edwin Bell, and Zachery Daniel Smith. Along with our daughters and granddaughter, they're our greatest treasures.

Ginger and FatCat
Sharing a Father-Daughter moment

JoDanna and Jiles
Our youngest daughter, and Grandson

OCTOBER 23, 2008

HUMAN CLONING & THE FUTURE OF MANKIND | **HIGH LIFE** TALLEST BUILDING

TIMES

The Woman Who Will Be Queen!

Papa's Little Princess

Jayda Nevaeh Eden Brumbaugh – our granddaughter. The only granddaughter we have so far, so you know she's not spoiled. ;-) Two years old on October 1, 2011.

"IN GOD WE TRUST!"

Made in the USA
Coppell, TX
15 October 2021